I0134382

The Legacy of Pope Leo

By Corey A. Chuba

VITAE PRESS
EMBARK ON YOUR QUEST

Copyright © 2025 by Corey A. Chuba

ISBN: 978-1-967470-08-2

Published by Vitae Press LLC

Cover design by Corey A. Chuba

All rights reserved.

This book is protected by copyright. No part of it may be
reproduced, stored in a retrieval system, or transmitted in
any form or by any means, electronic, mechanical,
photocopying, recording, or otherwise, without the prior
written permission of the publisher, except for brief
quotations used in reviews or critical articles.

Vitae Press

Vitae Press is a publishing house dedicated to exploring the enduring legacy of Western life, thought, and culture as shaped by the Roman tradition. The name *Vitae*, derived from the Latin word for "life," reflects our mission to publish works that engage with the values, ideas, and heritage of the Western world. From fiction to non-fiction to reprints of timeless works from Christendom and Western Civilization, each book seeks to deepen the understanding of the moral, spiritual, and intellectual foundations that have guided generations and continue to inspire today.

TABLE OF CONTENTS

The Legacy of Pope Leo

ACKNOWLEDGMENTS

I would like to thank my parents, Leonard and Marnie Chuba, for raising me in the sacramental life of the Catholic Church—the one true Church established by Our Lord Jesus Christ in the Gospels and handed down through the apostles and their successors. From my earliest days, I was brought to the confessional to receive absolution for my sins and to the altar to receive the true and living presence of Christ in the Most Holy Eucharist. It is within this one Body of Christ, outside of which there is no salvation, that I have found truth, beauty, and goodness. That which is severed from this Body will perish, but in it we are nourished and sustained unto eternal life. This work is dedicated in gratitude to that sacred inheritance.

INTRODUCTION

Pope Leo XIV was elected on May 8, A.D. 2025, marking a historic moment as the first American pope in the history of the Catholic Church. This unprecedented event adds a new chapter to the rich and storied legacy of papacies that have borne the name *Leo*. Thirteen popes have carried this revered title, each leaving a distinct mark not only on the Church but on the broader world. The papacies of these Leos have spanned centuries, guiding the faithful through times of persecution, renewal, reform, and global change.

This is more than a story of names and dates—it is a continuation of the very foundation Christ laid when He said to St. Peter, *"And I tell you, you are Peter, and on this rock I will build my church, and the gates of Hades will not prevail against it" (Matthew 16:18)*. From that moment, the papacy has been the enduring center of Christian authority in the world. And for over a thousand years, especially through its embrace by the European Gentile world, the Catholic Church became the architect of Western Civilization. From monasteries and cathedrals to universities, hospitals, orphanages, and

Introduction

charitable institutions, the Church laid the groundwork for many of the blessings and institutions we take for granted today. The popes did not merely guide souls; they crowned kings, advised emperors, preserved learning through the Dark Ages, and helped shape the moral, intellectual, and political fabric of Europe and beyond.

In this book, we will journey through the lives and legacies of the thirteen popes who bore the name *Leo*, examining their individual stories and the times in which they lived. Though separated by centuries, many of these Leos shared common threads: a fierce commitment to the Gospel, courage in the face of heresy and upheaval, and an unwavering vision of unity in the Body of Christ.

We begin with **Pope Leo I**, also known as *Leo the Great*, whose papacy in the 5th-century A.D. laid much of the theological foundation for the Church that would endure through the ages. His writings, particularly his defense of the two natures of Christ in his *Tome of Leo*, played a decisive role at the Council of Chalcedon in A.D. 451. His successful diplomatic efforts—such as persuading Attila the Hun to turn back from Rome—added to his legendary status, securing his reputation as *one of the greatest popes in history*.

Pope Leo II, reigning in the 7th-century A.D., followed in the footsteps of his predecessors by defending orthodox doctrine. He confirmed the acts of the Third Council of Constantinople, condemning monothelitism, and helped ensure doctrinal clarity during a time of lingering Christological controversy.

Pope Leo III ascended the papal throne in A.D. 795 and played a pivotal role in shaping medieval Christendom. His most significant act was the coronation of Charlemagne as *Emperor of the Romans* on Christmas Day in A.D. 800. This act did not merely revive the Western Roman Empire; it firmly wedded the papacy to the fate of European political power and helped give rise to what would become the Holy Roman Empire.

Pope Leo IV, elected in the mid-9th-century A.D., was a builder and protector of Rome. He fortified the city's defenses after a Saracen raid, initiating the construction of the Leonine Wall. His dedication to strengthening Rome physically symbolized the Church's spiritual fortification during a time of external threat and instability.

Pope Leo V, though little is known of his brief and contested papacy in A.D. 903, represents the turbulence of the papal throne during the *saeculum obscurum*—an era marked by intense political interference in Church affairs.

Introduction

Pope Leo VI served during the early-10ᵗʰ-century A.D. His reign was short and largely ceremonial due to the dominance of secular Roman nobility in papal matters.

Pope Leo VII, who reigned from A.D. 936 to 939, was chosen by the Holy Roman Emperor Otto I and helped mediate between monastic reformers and secular authorities. His papacy illustrates the growing collaboration between popes and emperors in shaping Christendom.

Pope Leo VIII is among the most disputed popes in Church history, with his legitimacy questioned due to political manipulation by the emperor Otto I. Some sources label him an antipope, though he is now listed officially among the valid popes.

Pope Leo IX, who reigned from A.D. 1049 to 1054, is remembered as a reformer and a pivotal figure in the events leading to the East–West Schism. He sought to eradicate simony and clerical marriage, reinforcing the moral authority of the papacy. His confrontation with the Patriarch of Constantinople, while intended to restore unity, unfortunately resulted in the formal schism of the Eastern Orthodox churches from the Catholic Church.

Pope Leo X, led the Church during the height of the

Renaissance, a time of extraordinary artistic and intellectual renewal. A Medici by birth and a patron of great artists like Raphael and Michelangelo, Leo X sought to glorify God through beauty and learning. His pontificate witnessed the beginning of Martin Luther's protests, which would later develop into the Protestant Revolt. While the political and theological complexities of the time posed immense challenges, Leo X remained devoted to the unity and authority of the Church.

Pope Leo XI, sometimes called *Papa Lampo* ("Lightning Pope") due to the brevity of his reign—just 27 days in A.D. 1605—left little legacy due to his sudden death, though his election reflected the intense political maneuvering of early modern Europe.

Pope Leo XII, elected in A.D. 1823, governed the Church during the Restoration era following the Napoleonic upheavals. A conservative and disciplinarian, he attempted to reaffirm papal authority and Catholic identity in a rapidly changing world marked by growing secularism and nationalism.

Pope Leo XIII, reigning from A.D. 1878 to 1903, stands as one of the most influential modern popes. His landmark encyclical *Rerum Novarum* addressed the rights and duties of labor and capital, laying the foundation of Catholic social teaching. His intellectual engagement with modernity and his efforts to open dialogue with the modern world ensured that the Church would not retreat from social issues but seek to shape them with a moral compass.

The election of **Pope Leo XIV** in A.D. 2025 is not only a historical moment in the Church's ongoing journey but a deliberate statement of continuity, resolve, and hope for the future. By choosing the name Leo, the newly elected pontiff has embraced the weight and the legacy of his predecessors. This decision is particularly significant in a time when the Church is faced with unprecedented challenges. In the face of secularization, moral decline, and the fragmentation of faith worldwide, Pope Leo XIV's choice signals a deep commitment to returning to the theological roots that have long defined the strength and unity of the Church.

The name Leo carries with it an innate sense of responsibility, reminding the faithful that, like the Leos before him, the new pope is called to be both a spiritual leader and a moral authority in the world. Pope Leo XIV's selection of this name suggests his intention to engage deeply with the most pressing issues facing the Church today. Much like **Leo I**, who defended the faith from heresy, and **Leo XIII**, who fought for Catholic social teaching, the new Pope Leo seems poised to address both the internal health of the Church and the role of Catholics in a modern world that increasingly distances itself from religion.

In the following pages, we will explore the lives and papacies of each of the thirteen Pope Leos, reflecting on their unique contributions to the Church's enduring legacy. From the powerful theology of Leo the Great to the insightful social teachings of Leo XIII, and now, the hopeful and determined leadership of Pope Leo XIV, the name "Leo" will continue to inspire generations to come.

Corey A. Chuba
Pittsburgh, Pennsylvania
May, A.D. 2025

Introduction

A COMPLETE LIST OF THE POPES

1. **St. Peter** (A.D. 32-67)
2. **St. Linus** (A.D 67-76)
3. **St. Anacletus (Cletus)** (A.D. 76-88)
4. **St. Clement I** (A.D. 88-97)
5. **St. Evaristus** (A.D. 97-105)
6. **St. Alexander I** (A.D. 105-115)
7. **St. Sixtus I** (A.D. 115-125) (Also called Xystus I)
8. **St. Telesphorus** (A.D. 125-136)
9. **St. Hyginus** (A.D. 136-140)
10. **St. Pius I** (A.D. 140-155)
11. **St. Anicetus** (A.D. 155-166)
12. **St. Soter** (A.D. 166-175)
13. **St. Eleutherius** (A.D. 175-189)
14. **St. Victor I** (A.D. 189-199)
15. **St. Zephyrinus** (A.D. 199-217)
16. **St. Callistus I** (A.D. 217-222)
17. **St. Urban I** (A.D. 222-230)
18. **St. Pontain** (A.D. 230-235)
19. **St. Anterus** (A.D. 235-236)
20. **St. Fabian** (A.D. 236-250)
21. **St. Cornelius** (A.D. 251-253)
22. **St. Lucius I** (A.D. 253-254)
23. **St. Stephen I** (A.D. 254-257)
24. **St. Sixtus II** (A.D. 257-258)
25. **St. Dionysius** (A.D. 259-268)
26. **St. Felix I** (A.D. 269-274)
27. **St. Eutychian** (A.D. 275-283)
28. **St. Caius (Gaius)** (A.D. 283-296)
29. **St. Marcellinus** (A.D. 296-304)
30. **St. Marcellus I** (A.D. 308-309)
31. **St. Eusebius** (A.D. 309 or 310)
32. **St. Miltiades** (A.D. 311-314)
33. **St. Sylvester I** (A.D. 314-335)
34. **St. Marcus** (A.D. 336)
35. **St. Julius I** (A.D. 337-352)
36. **Liberius** (A.D. 352-366)
37. **St. Damasus I** (A.D. 366-383)
38. **St. Siricius** (A.D. 384-399)
39. **St. Anastasius I** (A.D. 399-401)
40. **St. Innocent I** (A.D. 401-417)
41. **St. Zosimus** (A.D. 417-418)
42. **St. Boniface I** (A.D. 418-422)
43. **St. Celestine I** (A.D. 422-432)
44. **St. Sixtus III** (A.D. 432-440)
45. **St. Leo I (the Great)** (A.D. 440-461)
46. **St. Hilarius** (A.D. 461-468)
47. **St. Simplicius** (A.D. 468-483)
48. **St. Felix III (II)** (A.D. 483-492)

A Complete List of the Popes

49. **St. Gelasius I** (A.D. 492-496)
50. **Anastasius II** (A.D. 496-498)
51. **St. Symmachus** (A.D. 498-514)
52. **St. Hormisdas** (A.D. 514-523)
53. **St. John I** (A.D. 523-526)
54. **St. Felix IV (III)** (A.D. 526-530)
55. **Boniface II** (A.D. 530-532)
56. **John II** (A.D. 533-535)
57. **St. Agapetus I** (A.D. 535-536)
58. **St. Silverius** (A.D. 536-537)
59. **Vigilius** (A.D. 537-555)
60. **Pelagius I** (A.D. 556-561)
61. **John III** (A.D. 561-574)
62. **Benedict I** (A.D. 575-579)
63. **Pelagius II** (A.D. 579-590)
64. **St. Gregory I (the Great)** (A.D. 590-604)
65. **Sabinian** (A.D. 604-606)
66. **Boniface III** (A.D. 607)
67. **St. Boniface IV** (A.D. 608-615)
68. **St. Deusdedit (Adeodatus I)** (A.D. 615-618)
69. **Boniface V** (A.D. 619-625)
70. **Honorius I** (A.D. 625-638)
71. **Severinus** (A.D. 640)
72. **John IV** (A.D. 640-642)
73. **Theodore I** (A.D. 642-649)
74. **St. Martin I** (A.D. 649-655)
75. **St. Eugene I** (A.D. 655-657)
76. **St. Vitalian** (A.D. 657-672)
77. **Adeodatus II** (A.D. 672-676)
78. **Donus** (A.D. 676-678)
79. **St. Agatho** (A.D. 678-681)
80. **St. Leo II** (A.D. 682-683)
81. **St. Benedict II** (A.D. 684-685)
82. **John V** (A.D. 685-686)
83. **Conon** (A.D. 686-687)
84. **St. Sergius I** (A.D. 687-701)
85. **John VI** (A.D. 701-705)
86. **John VII** (A.D. 705-707)
87. **Sisinnius** (A.D. 708)
88. **Constantine** (A.D. 708-715)
89. **St. Gregory II** (A.D. 715-731)
90. **St. Gregory III** (A.D. 731-741)
91. **St. Zachary** (A.D. 741-752)
92. **Stephen II** (A.D. 752-757)
93. **St. Paul I** (A.D. 757-767)
94. **St. Stephen III** (A.D. 768-772)
95. **Adrian I** (A.D. 772-795)
96. **St. Leo III** (A.D. 795-816)
97. **Stephen IV** (A.D. 816-817)
98. **St. Paschal I** (A.D. 817-824)
99. **Eugene II** (A.D. 824-827)
100. **Valentine** (A.D. 827)
101. **Gregory IV** (A.D. 827-844)
102. **Sergius II** (A.D. 844-847)
103. **St. Leo IV** (A.D. 847-855)
104. **Benedict III** (A.D. 855-858)
105. **St. Nicholas I (The Great)** (A.D. 858-867)
106. **Adrian II** (A.D. 867-872)
107. **John VIII** (A.D. 872-882)
108. **Marinus I** (A.D. 882-884)
109. **St. Adrian III** (A.D. 884-885)
110. **Stephen V** (A.D. 885-891)
111. **Formosus** (A.D. 891-896)
112. **Boniface VI** (A.D. 896)

113. **Stephen VI** (A.D. 896-897)
114. **Romanus** (A.D. 897)
115. **Theodore II** (A.D. 897)
116. **John IX** (A.D. 898-900)
117. **Benedict IV** (A.D. 900-903)
118. **Leo V** (A.D. 903)
119. **Sergius III** (A.D. 904-911)
120. **Anastasius III** (A.D. 911-913)
121. **Lando** (A.D. 913-914)
122. **John X** (A.D. 914-928)
123. **Leo VI** (A.D. 928)
124. **Stephen VII** (A.D. 929-931)
125. **John XI** (A.D. 931-935)
126. **Leo VII** (A.D. 936-939)
127. **Stephen VIII** (A.D. 939-942)
128. **Marinus II** (A.D. 942-946)
129. **Agapetus II** (A.D. 946-955)
130. **John XII** (A.D. 955-963)
131. **Leo VIII** (A.D. 963-964)
132. **Benedict V** (A.D. 964)
133. **John XIII** (A.D. 965-972)
134. **Benedict VI** (A.D. 973-974)
135. **Benedict VII** (A.D. 974-983)
136. **John XIV** (A.D. 983-984)
137. **John XV** (A.D. 985-996)
138. **Gregory V** (A.D. 996-999)
139. **Sylvester II** (A.D. 999-1003)
140. **John XVII** (A.D. 1003)
141. **John XVIII** (A.D. 1003-1009)
142. **Sergius IV** (A.D. 1009-1012)
143. **Benedict VIII** (A.D. 1012-1024)
144. **John XIX** (A.D. 1024-1032)
145. **Benedict IX** (A.D. 1032-1045)

- Appears on the list three times due to being deposed and restored
146. **Sylvester III** (A.D. 1045)
147. **Benedict IX** (A.D. 1045)
148. **Gregory VI** (A.D. 1045-1046)
149. **Clement II** (A.D. 1046-1047)
150. **Benedict IX** (A.D. 1047-1048)
151. **Damasus II** (A.D. 1048)
152. **St. Leo IX** (A.D. 1049-1054)
153. **Victor II** (A.D. 1055-1057)
154. **Stephen IX** (A.D. 1057-1058)
155. **Nicholas II** (A.D. 1058-1061)
156. **Alexander II** (A.D. 1061-1073)
157. **St. Gregory VII** (A.D. 1073-1085)
158. **Blessed Victor III** (A.D. 1086-1087)
159. **Blessed Urban II** (A.D. 1088-1099)
160. **Paschal II** (A.D. 1099-1118)
161. **Gelasius II** (A.D. 1118-1119)
162. **Callistus II** (A.D. 1119-1124)
163. **Honorius II** (A.D. 1124-1130)
164. **Innocent II** (A.D. 1130-1143)
165. **Celestine II** (A.D. 1143-1144)
166. **Lucius II** (A.D. 1144-1145)
167. **Blessed Eugene III** (A.D. 1145-1153)

168. **Anastasius IV** (A.D. 1153-1154)
169. **Adrian IV** (A.D. 1154-1159)
170. **Alexander III** (A.D. 1159-1181)
171. **Lucius III** (A.D. 1181-1185)
172. **Urban III** (A.D. 1185-1187)
173. **Gregory VIII** (A.D. 1187)
174. **Clement III** (A.D. 1187-1191)
175. **Celestine III** (A.D. 1191–1198)
176. **Innocent III** (A.D. 1198–1216)
177. **Honorius III** (A.D. 1216–1227)
178. **Gregory IX** (A.D. 1227–1241)
179. **Celestine IV** (A.D. 1241)
180. **Innocent IV** (A.D. 1243–1254)
181. **Alexander IV** (A.D. 1254–1261)
182. **Urban IV** (A.D. 1261–1264)
183. **Clement IV** (A.D. 1265–1268)

- After the death of Clement IV, there was a three-year **interregnum** without a valid pope (A.D. 1268-1271).

184. **Blessed Gregory X** (A.D. 1271–1276)
185. **Blessed Innocent V** (A.D. 1276)
186. **Adrian V** (A.D. 1276)
187. **John XXI** (A.D. 1276–1277)
188. **Nicholas III** (A.D. 1277–1280)
189. **Martin IV** (A.D. 1281–1285)
190. **Honorius IV** (A.D. 1285–1287)
191. **Nicholas IV** (A.D. 1288–1292)

- After the death of Nicholas IV, there was a two-year **interregnum** without a valid pope (A.D. 1292-1294).

192. **St. Celestine V** (A.D. 1294)
193. **Boniface VIII** (A.D. 1294–1303)
194. **Blessed Benedict XI** (A.D. 1303–1304)
195. **Clement V** (A.D. 1305–1314)

- After the death of Clement V, there was a two-year **interregnum** without a valid pope (A.D. 1314-1316).

196. **John XXII** (A.D. 1316–1334)
197. **Benedict XII** (A.D. 1334–1342)
198. **Clement VI** (A.D. 1342–1352)
199. **Innocent VI** (A.D. 1352–1362)
200. **Blessed Urban V** (A.D. 1362–1370)
201. **Gregory XI** (A.D. 1370–1378)
202. **Urban VI** (A.D. 1378–1389)
203. **Boniface IX** (A.D. 1389–1404)
204. **Innocent VII** (A.D. 1404–1406)

205. **Gregory XII** (A.D. 1406–1415)
- After the death of Gregory XII, there was a two-year **interregnum** without a valid pope (A.D. 1415-1417).

206. **Martin V** (A.D. 1417–1431)
207. **Eugene IV** (A.D. 1431–1447)
208. **Nicholas V** (A.D. 1447–1455)
209. **Callistus III** (A.D. 1455–1458)
210. **Pius II** (A.D. 1458–1464)
211. **Paul II** (A.D. 1464–1471)
212. **Sixtus IV** (A.D. 1471–1484)
213. **Innocent VIII** (A.D. 1484–1492)
214. **Alexander VI** (A.D. 1492–1503)
215. **Pius III** (A.D. 1503)
216. **Julius II** (A.D. 1503–1513)
217. **Leo X** (A.D. 1513–1521)
218. **Adrian VI** (A.D. 1522–1523)
219. **Clement VII** (A.D. 1523–1534)
220. **Paul III** (A.D. 1534–1549)
221. **Julius III** (A.D. 1550–1555)
222. **Marcellus II** (A.D. 1555)
223. **Paul IV** (A.D. 1555–1559)
224. **Pius IV** (A.D. 1559–1565)
225. **St. Pius V** (A.D. 1566–1572)
226. **Gregory XIII** (A.D. 1572–1585)
227. **Sixtus V** (A.D. 1585–1590)
228. **Urban VII** (A.D. 1590)
229. **Gregory XIV** (A.D. 1590–1591)
230. **Innocent IX** (A.D. 1591)
231. **Clement VIII** (A.D. 1592–1605)
232. **Leo XI** (A.D. 1605)
233. **Paul V** (A.D. 1605–1621)
234. **Gregory XV** (A.D. 1621–1623)
235. **Urban VIII** (A.D. 1623–1644)
236. **Innocent X** (A.D. 1644–1655)
237. **Alexander VII** (A.D. 1655–1667)
238. **Clement IX** (A.D. 1667–1669)
239. **Clement X** (A.D. 1670–1676)
240. **Blessed Innocent XI** (A.D. 1676–1689)
241. **Alexander VIII** (A.D. 1689–1691)
242. **Innocent XII** (A.D. 1691–1700)
243. **Clement XI** (A.D. 1700–1721)
244. **Innocent XIII** (A.D. 1721–1724)
245. **Benedict XIII** (A.D. 1724–1730)
246. **Clement XII** (A.D. 1730–1740)
247. **Benedict XIV** (A.D. 1740–1758)
248. **Clement XIII** (A.D. 1758–1769)
249. **Clement XIV** (A.D. 1769–1774)
250. **Pius VI** (A.D. 1775–1799)
- After the death of Pius VI, there was a 6-month **interregnum** without a valid pope (A.D. 1799-1800).

251. **Pius VII** (A.D. 1800–1823)
252. **Leo XII** (A.D. 1823–1829)

A Complete List of the Popes

253. **Pius VIII** (A.D. 1829–1830)
254. **Gregory XVI** (A.D. 1831–1846)
255. **Blessed Pius IX** (A.D. 1846–1878)
256. **Leo XIII** (A.D. 1878–1903)
257. **St. Pius X** (A.D. 1903–1914)
258. **Benedict XV** (A.D. 1914–1922)
259. **Pius XI** (A.D. 1922–1939)
260. **Pius XII** (A.D. 1939–1958)
261. **St. John XXIII** (A.D. 1958–1963)
262. **Paul VI** (A.D. 1963–1978)
263. **John Paul I** (A.D. 1978)
264. **St. John Paul II** (A.D. 1978–2005)
265. **Benedict XVI** (A.D. 2005–2013)
266. **Francis** (A.D. 2013-2025)
267. **Leo XIV** (A.D. 2025–present)

THE LEGACY OF POPE LEO

Thirteen Popes that Shaped the Church and the World

Chapter I

Pope Leo I (A.D. 440-461)

A Pillar of the Early Church

The exact place and date of Leo's birth remain unknown,

though the *Liber Pontificalis*[1] records that he was a native of Tuscany

and the son of a man named Quintianus. He was born with the name

Leo, which he retained upon ascending to the papacy. He died on 10

November, A.D. 461 after a momentous twenty-one-year reign as the

45th Bishop of Rome.

---

[1] **Liber Pontificalis:** (Latin for "Book of the Popes"), is a key collection of papal biographies that began in the late-5th-century A.D., traditionally attributed to clerical authors in Rome. While the earliest entries draw upon earlier sources such as the *Catalogus Liberianus* and the Roman *Depositio Martyrum*, the work expanded over time, with later continuations added well into the Renaissance. Though occasionally shaped by hagiographic or political motives, the *Liber Pontificalis* remains an indispensable source for reconstructing early papal chronology, ecclesiastical developments, and the material culture of Early Christianity.

> [Davis, Raymond. *The Book of Pontiffs (Liber Pontificalis): The Ancient Biographies of the First Ninety Roman Bishops to A.D. 715, Translated Texts for Historians, Vol. 6.* (Liverpool University Press, A.D. 1989), pp. 17-25.]

Pope Leo I

Leo's pontificate stands alongside that of St. Gregory the Great, as one of the most consequential in the history of early Christianity. He led the Church at a time of immense upheaval: the Western Roman Empire was crumbling, and the Eastern Church was embroiled in theological controversy, particularly surrounding the nature of Christ. In the midst of this turmoil, Leo emerged as a figure of remarkable clarity, strength, and vision—shaping not only the destiny of the Roman See but also that of the Universal Church.

Our earliest reliable records show Leo serving as a deacon under *Pope Celestine I*[2] (A.D. 422–432). Even then, his influence extended beyond Rome. Around A.D. 430 or 431, the theologian *John Cassian*[3] wrote his treatise *De Incarnatione Domini contra Nestorium* ("On

---

[2] **Pope Celestine I:** (reigned A.D. 422–432), was a vigorous defender of orthodoxy during a time of intense Christological debate. He condemned the teachings of Nestorius and played a decisive role in the events leading to the Council of Ephesus (A.D. 431), where the title *Theotokos* ("God-bearer") for Mary was dogmatically affirmed. Celestine also commissioned Palladius and, according to later tradition, St. Patrick, to evangelize the Irish, initiating Rome's missionary outreach to the British Isles.
 [Kelly, J.N.D. *The Oxford Dictionary of Popes.* (Oxford University Press, A.D. 1986), pp. 43–45.]
[3] **John Cassian:** (A.D. 360–435), born in Scythia Minor, traveled through Egypt to learn from the Desert Fathers before settling in Gaul. His major works—*De institutis coenobiorum* (Institutes) and *Collationes* (Conferences)—introduced Eastern ascetic ideals to Western monasticism, particularly in southern Gaul. Though his views on grace were later criticized in the context of the Pelagian controversy, Cassian's balanced spiritual theology profoundly influenced Benedict of Nursia and the Rule of St. Benedict.

the Incarnation of the Lord Against Nestorius") at Leo's request,

dedicating the work to him. This not only reveals Leo's early

engagement in Christological debates but also his growing stature in

the wider Christian world.

At the same time, the powerful *Patriarch Cyril of Alexandria*[4]

appealed to Rome concerning the jurisdictional overreach of *Bishop*

Juvenal of Jerusalem[5]—an indication that even before his papacy, Leo

was involved in resolving conflicts affecting the universal Church.

Though it's unclear whether Cyril addressed Leo directly as a deacon

or was writing to Pope Celestine, Leo later referenced this appeal in

his own letters (*Epistle 116*).

[Chadwick, Owen. *Western Asceticism*. (Library of Christian Classics, Westminster Press, A.D. 1958), pp. 199–235.]

[4] **Patriarch Cyril of Alexandria:** (A.D. 376–444), stands as a central figure in early Christological theology and ecclesiastical politics. As Patriarch from A.D. 412 until his death, he was a vigorous opponent of Nestorius, Archbishop of Constantinople, whose teachings he saw as dividing Christ's person. Cyril presided at the Council of Ephesus in A.D. 431, where the title *Theotokos* ("God-bearer") was affirmed for Mary, and Nestorius was formally condemned. His extensive theological writings shaped the Christological tradition of both Eastern and Western Christianity.

[McGuckin, John. *St. Cyril of Alexandria: The Christological Controversy*. (Brill, A.D. 1994), pp. 123–165.]

[5] **Bishop Juvenal of Jerusalem:** (reigned A.D. 422–458), played a pivotal role in advancing the status of the see of Jerusalem during the 5th-century A.D. Although traditionally subordinate to the metropolitan see of Caesarea and the patriarchate of Antioch, Juvenal sought and ultimately secured Jerusalem's elevation to a patriarchate at the Council of Chalcedon (A.D. 451).

[Price, Richard and Gaddis, Michael. *The Acts of the Council of Chalcedon, Vol. 1*. (Liverpool University Press, A.D. 2005), pp. 20–22, 86–89.]

Pope Leo I

Leo's administrative skill was not confined to ecclesiastical

matters. During the reign of *Pope Sixtus III*[6] (A.D. 432–440), the

Western Roman *Emperor Valentinian III*[7] entrusted him with a

sensitive diplomatic mission: to mediate a conflict in *Gaul*[8] between

---

[6] **Pope Sixtus III:** (reigned A.D. 432–440), the 44th bishop of Rome, played a pivotal role in consolidating doctrinal orthodoxy during a time of significant theological conflict. His papacy came in the aftermath of the Council of Ephesus (A.D. 431), and he actively upheld the condemnation of Nestorianism while also opposing Pelagianism. A notable patron of ecclesiastical architecture, Sixtus oversaw the construction and dedication of the Basilica of Santa Maria Maggiore (St. Mary Major), one of the oldest churches in the West dedicated to the Virgin Mary.

> [Kelly, J.N.D. *The Oxford Dictionary of Popes.* (Oxford: Oxford University Press, A.D. 1986), pp. 43–44.]

[7] **Emperor Valentinian III:** (reigned A.D. 425–455), ruled the Western Roman Empire during a period of accelerating decline. Ascending to the throne as a child under the regency of his mother, Galla Placidia, his reign was dominated by strong court officials and military generals, particularly the powerful magister militum Flavius Aetius. Valentinian presided over a crumbling empire beset by internal weakness and external threats, including invasions by the Huns, Vandals, and other Germanic tribes. His assassination in A.D. 455 marked a turning point in the final unravelling of Western Roman imperial authority.

> [Honore, Tony. *Law in the Crisis of Empire 379–455 AD: The Theodosian Dynasty and Its Quaestors.* (Oxford: Oxford University Press, A.D. 1998), pp. 239–243.]

[8] **Gaul:** (Latin: *Gallia*), was a major province of the Roman Empire encompassing the territories of modern France and extending into parts of Belgium, western Germany, northern Italy, and Switzerland. By the 5th-century A.D., Gaul was both strategically vital and deeply contested, facing waves of migration and invasion from groups such as the Visigoths, Franks, and Huns. The Battle of the Catalaunian Plains (A.D. 451), fought near modern-day Châlons-en-Champagne, was a turning point, as Roman general Flavius Aëtius led a coalition that successfully halted Attila the Hun's incursion.

> [Bury, J.B. *History of the Later Roman Empire, Vol. 1.* (New York: Dover Publications, A.D. 1958), pp. 325–329.]

the powerful general *Flavius Aëtius*[9] and the magistrate *Albinus*.[10] That

the imperial court selected Leo for such a task testifies to the

extraordinary confidence placed in his judgment, diplomacy, and

intellect.

While Leo was still in Gaul, Pope Sixtus III died on 19

August, A.D. 440. The Roman clergy and people unanimously elected

Leo as his successor. Upon returning to Rome, Leo was consecrated

as Bishop of Rome on 29 September, A.D. 440. Over the next two

decades, he would become a central figure in defining orthodoxy,

asserting papal authority, and preserving the unity of the Church

amid heresy and imperial decline.

---

[9] **Flavius Aëtius:** (A.D. 390–454), was one of the last great military commanders
of the Western Roman Empire. A seasoned general and diplomat, Aëtius was
instrumental in maintaining imperial authority during its twilight years. Known as
the last of the Romans, he famously orchestrated the defense of Gaul against the Huns
by forging an alliance with Visigothic forces and securing a critical victory at the
Battle of the Catalaunian Plains. His assassination by Emperor Valentinian III in
A.D. 454 removed one of the last stabilizing forces in the West.
    [Hughes, Ian. *Aetius: Attila's Nemesis.* (Barnsley: Pen & Sword Military,
        A.D. 2012), pp. 1–11, 175–200.]
[10] **Albinus:** properly *Decimus Clodius Albinus* (A.D. 150–197), was a Roman general
and senator who declared himself emperor during the turbulent Year of the Five
Emperors (A.D. 193). Initially aligned with Septimius Severus against the usurper
Pescennius Niger, Albinus was later proclaimed emperor by his troops in Britain
and Gaul. He ultimately clashed with Severus for control of the empire and was
defeated and killed at the Battle of Lugdunum in A.D. 197.
    [Birley, Anthony R. *Septimius Severus: The African Emperor.* (London:
        Routledge, A.D. 1988), pp. 102–122.]

Defender of Orthodoxy and Guardian of Church Unity

Leo's foremost concern as pope was to preserve the unity

and doctrinal integrity of the Church. Shortly after his elevation to

the Chair of St. Peter, he was drawn into active conflict with several

heresies that threatened to fracture the Western Church. His

response was swift, decisive, and rooted in a profound sense of

pastoral duty.

One of his earliest challenges came from remnants of the

Pelagian heresy.[11] Through *Bishop Septimus of Altinum,*[12] Leo learned that

in the region of *Aquileia,*[13] former followers of Pelagius—including

---

[11] **Pelagian heresy:** originated with the teachings of Pelagius, a British monk active in Rome and North Africa during the late-4th- and early-5th-centuries A.D. Pelagius rejected the doctrine of original sin and asserted that human beings possessed the natural ability to choose good without the necessity of divine grace. His teachings were sharply opposed by St. Augustine of Hippo, who emphasized the fallen state of humanity and the indispensable role of grace in salvation. Pelagianism was condemned at several synods, most notably the Council of Carthage in A.D. 418, and declared heretical by Pope Zosimus in A.D. 418–419.

 [Bonner, Gerald. *St. Augustine of Hippo: Life and Controversies.* (Norwich: Canterbury Press, A.D. 2002), pp. 335–354.]

[12] **Bishop Septimus of Altinum:** was a lesser-known but important episcopal figure in northern Italy during the mid-5th-century A.D. He is chiefly remembered for his correspondence with Pope Leo I, in which he warned of the spread of Pelagianism in the ecclesiastical province of Aquileia. Leo responded by organizing a synod to reaffirm the condemnation of the heresy and enforce doctrinal orthodoxy among the northern Italian churches.

 [Hefele, Charles Joseph. *A History of the Councils of the Church, Vol. 3, trans. William Clark.* (Edinburgh: T&T Clark, A.D. 1896), pp. 290–293.]

[13] **Aquileia:** located near the northern Adriatic coast in modern-day Italy, was one of the most prominent cities in the Roman Empire, both militarily and ecclesiastically. By the 5th-century A.D., it had developed into a major center of Christianity and was recognized as a patriarchate by the mid-6th-century A.D.

priests, deacons, and other clerics—were being readmitted to communion without any formal renunciation of their errors. Deeply troubled by this leniency, Leo issued a sharp rebuke. He ordered the convening of a provincial synod in Aquileia, insisting that all those previously aligned with Pelagianism publicly abjure the heresy and formally subscribe to a clear confession of orthodox faith. Pope Leo I references these events in his letters (*Epistles 1 and 2*).

Even more vigorously did Leo confront the spread of Manichaeism—a dualistic and syncretic religion that had already been condemned by earlier Church authorities. Driven out of North Africa by the Vandal invasions, many Manichaean adherents had taken refuge in Rome, quietly establishing a clandestine community. Leo, recognizing the spiritual danger they posed, did not hesitate to act. He urged the faithful to report known Manichaeans to their priests and, in A.D. 443, led a public investigation alongside Roman senators and clergy. The leaders of the sect were interrogated, and Leo issued

---

During the papacy of Leo I, Aquileia became a focal point in the struggle against Pelagianism and other theological controversies. The city was also noted for its resistance against invading forces such as Attila the Hun, who sacked Aquileia in A.D. 452.

      [Heather, Peter. *The Fall of the Roman Empire: A New History*. (Oxford: Oxford University Press, A.D. 2006), pp. 361–364.]

repeated warnings in his sermons, cautioning the people of Rome against the subtle allure of this heresy. From Pope Leo's published sermons, we know that he instructed Christians to report the whereabouts, associates, and meeting places of the Manichaean believers.

As a result of his efforts, some Manichaeans were converted and reconciled to the Church through confession. Those who remained obstinate were handed over to the civil authorities and, in accordance with imperial law, were banished from the city. On 30 January, A.D. 444, Leo sent a circular letter (*Epistle 7*) to all the bishops of Italy, enclosing the records of his actions against the sect in Rome and urging them to be vigilant against its spread.

Leo's influence extended into imperial policy as well. On 19 June, A.D. 445, Emperor Valentinian III—likely acting under Leo's counsel—issued a harsh edict instituting seven penalties against the Manichaeans (*Epistle 8*). The pope's campaign against the heresy proved so effective that, according to *Prosper of Aquitaine*[14] in his

---

[14] **Prosper of Aquitaine:** (A.D. 390–455), was a Christian writer and historian from Gaul. He is best known for his Chronicle, a work that provides valuable historical information about the events of the 5th-century A.D., particularly concerning the theology and politics of the time. Prosper was a staunch defender of

Chronicle, the Manichaeans were driven out not only from Rome but also from the surrounding provinces. Eastern bishops even began to imitate Leo's methods, demonstrating the wide reach of his leadership.

Meanwhile, in Spain, another heretical movement known as *Priscillianism*[15] continued to smolder. Though condemned decades earlier, it still found new adherents. *Bishop Turibius of Astorga*[16] took it upon himself to investigate the spread of the heresy throughout the Spanish churches. After documenting the sect's doctrines and

---

the teachings of St. Augustine and was an ally of Pope Leo I in combating heresies such as Manichaeism.

> [Prosper of Aquitaine. *Chronicle, trans. A. C. Murray in From Roman to Merovingian Gaul: A Reader.* (Toronto: University of Toronto Press, A.D. 1999), pp. 47–58.]

[15] **Priscillianism:** was a heterodox Christian movement founded by Priscillian, Bishop of Ávila in Hispania, during the late-4th-century A.D. The movement fused elements of Gnosticism, Manichaean dualism, and a rigorist ascetic lifestyle, emphasizing a spiritual elitism and secret interpretation of Scripture. Condemned by the Council of Saragossa in A.D. 380 and denounced as heretical by Church authorities, Priscillian became the first Christian executed for heresy under civil law in A.D. 385. Despite this, his followers endured well into the 6th-century A.D., particularly in Galicia and Lusitania.

> [Chadwick, Henry. *Priscillian of Avila: The Occult and the Charismatic in the Early Church.* (Oxford: Clarendon Press, A.D. 1976), pp. 1–57.]

[16] **Bishop Turibius of Astorga:** was a leading ecclesiastical figure in Hispania known for his unwavering campaign against the Priscillianist sect, which remained active in northwestern Spain long after its founder's death. In a preserved letter to Pope Leo I, Turibius outlined the persistence of heretical doctrines in his diocese and requested papal support. In response, Leo issued a letter of commendation and condemnation of the sect in A.D. 447.

> [Collins, Roger. *Visigothic Spain 409–711.* (Oxford: Blackwell, A.D. 2004), pp. 27–28.]

refuting them in writing, he sent his findings to several African

bishops—and also to Leo himself.

In response, Leo composed a lengthy and theologically robust

letter (*Epistle 15*) refuting the errors of the Priscillianists. He

instructed Turibius to convene a council of bishops from nearby

provinces to conduct a rigorous inquiry, specifically to determine

whether any bishops had themselves become compromised by the

heresy. Any such individuals, Leo declared, were to be

excommunicated without delay.

Additionally, Leo wrote to the bishops of the Spanish

provinces, urging the convocation of a general synod to address the

matter. If a full synod was not feasible, then at the very least, the

bishops of *Galicia*[17] were to be assembled. These councils did in fact

take place and addressed the concerns Leo had raised, reaffirming his

---

[17] **Galicia:** a region in the northwestern Iberian Peninsula encompassing parts of
modern-day Spain and Portugal, was an important ecclesiastical province in Late
Antiquity. By the 5th-century A.D., Galicia had a well-established Christian presence
with multiple dioceses, including Astorga and Braga, that actively participated in
doctrinal disputes such as those concerning Priscillianism and Pelagianism. Bishops
from this region were regularly involved in synods and correspondence with Rome,
including letters to Pope Leo I, reflecting the region's integration into broader
theological currents of the Latin Church.
    [Collins, Roger. *Early Medieval Spain: Unity in Diversity, 400–1000*. (New
York: St. Martin's Press, A.D. 1983), pp. 52–58.]

role not only as the Bishop of Rome but as a central figure in guiding the wider Church.

Papal Authority and Episcopal Autonomy

The widespread disorganization of the Church in certain regions—brought about by ongoing national migrations—required a stronger connection between local episcopates and Rome in order to stabilize and advance ecclesiastical life. With this goal in mind, Pope Leo the Great sought to strengthen the authority of the papal vicariate in Gaul by supporting the bishops of *Arles*[18] as a unifying center for the Gallican Church in direct communion with the Holy See.

However, Leo's efforts faced serious challenges, particularly in his contentious relationship with *St. Hilary,*[19] then Bishop of Arles.

---

[18] **Arles:** located in southern Gaul, served as one of the most influential ecclesiastical centers in the Western Roman Empire during Late Antiquity. As the seat of a metropolitan archbishopric, Arles exerted jurisdictional authority over a wide region of southern Gaul. Its prominence was bolstered by imperial support and proximity to trade routes, allowing it to become a focal point of theological discourse, church governance, and monastic reform. The see of Arles frequently mediated disputes among provincial churches and was at times a rival to other major sees such as Vienne and Milan.

> [Mathisen, Ralph. *Roman Aristocrats in Barbarian Gaul: Strategies for Survival in an Age of Transition.* (Austin: University of Texas Press, A.D. 1993), pp. 141–145.]

[19] **St. Hilary:** (A.D. 403–449), a relative of St. Honoratus, succeeded him as Bishop of Arles and became a champion of ascetic and monastic ideals within the Gallican Church. Renowned for his personal austerity and pastoral zeal, Hilary also

Pope Leo I

Disputes over the authority and privileges of the Arlesian vicariate had already surfaced before Leo's time, but under Hilary's leadership, tensions escalated. Hilary claimed jurisdictional authority over multiple ecclesiastical provinces and asserted that all episcopal consecrations in the region should be conducted by him, rather than by their respective metropolitans.

One notable conflict arose when *Bishop Celidonius*[20] of Besançon was accused of being unfit for episcopal office—allegedly for having married a widow while still a layman, and for sanctioning a death sentence in his role as a public official. Acting unilaterally, St.

---

exercised vigorous metropolitan oversight, appointing bishops and intervening in ecclesiastical disputes. This assertiveness brought him into conflict with Pope Leo I, who viewed such autonomy as overreach. In A.D. 445, Leo secured an imperial rescript from Emperor Valentinian III limiting Hilary's jurisdiction and reinforcing papal primacy in the West.

> [Pope Leo I. *Epistola 10 (To the Bishops of the Province of Vienne)*, in *Patrologia Latina*, ed. J.-P. Migne, Vol. 54; Dam, Raymond Van. *Saints and Their Miracles in Late Antique Gaul.* (Princeton: Princeton University Press, A.D. 1993), pp. 109–113.]

[20] **Bishop Celidonius:** served as bishop of Besançon in eastern Gaul during the mid-5th-century A.D. His episcopacy became the center of a landmark dispute concerning ecclesiastical jurisdiction. St. Hilary of Arles deposed Celidonius on grounds of prior misconduct—reportedly for having served as a magistrate and being married before his ordination. Celidonius appealed directly to Pope Leo I, who held a hearing in Rome and ultimately reinstated him, thereby asserting papal authority in provincial disputes and establishing a precedent for appeals to the Roman See.

> [Pope Leo I. *Epistola 10 and Epistola 12 (To the Bishops of the Province of Vienne and on Celidonius)*, in *Patrologia Latina*, ed. J.-P. Migne, Vol. 54; Dunn, Geoffrey D. *Leo the Great.* (London: Routledge, A.D. 2007), pp. 73–78.]

The Legacy of Pope Leo

Hilary deposed Celidonius and appointed *Importunus*[21] as his successor. Celidonius, in response, appealed directly to Pope Leo and traveled to Rome to plead his case.

Simultaneously, St. Hilary had also consecrated a new bishop for the see of *Bishop Projectus,*[22] who was gravely ill. When Projectus unexpectedly recovered, he too filed a complaint with the papacy over Hilary's overreach.

Pope Leo convened a Roman synod around A.D. 445 to address these disputes. When the charges against Celidonius could not be substantiated, Leo reinstated him in his episcopal office.

---

[21] **Importunus:** was appointed by St. Hilary of Arles as bishop of Besançon following the contested deposition of Celidonius. His installation without Roman approval exacerbated tensions between the Gallican episcopate and Pope Leo I, who viewed such actions as a violation of established ecclesiastical norms. The controversy surrounding Importunus illustrates the wider struggle between regional autonomy in Gaul and the centralizing tendencies of the Roman papacy during the 5th-century A.D.

[Dam, R. Van. *Leadership and Community in Late Antique Gaul.* (Berkeley: University of California Press, A.D. 1985), pp. 105–108; Pope Leo I. *Epistola 12,* in *Patrologia Latina,* ed. J.-P. Migne, Vol. 54.]

[22] **Bishop Projectus:** a less well-known Gallic prelate of the mid-5th-century A.D., appears in correspondence involving Pope Leo I and the activities of Hilary of Arles. Projectus's case contributed to the growing papal concerns over Hilary's episcopal interventions, as Leo sought to curb unauthorized appointments and consolidate Roman primacy over regional ecclesiastical governance. Though details are sparse, Projectus represents one of several bishops whose careers were shaped by the shifting balance of authority between local metropolitans and the Roman pontiff.

[Dunn, Geoffrey D. *Leo the Great and the Spiritual Rebuilding of a Universal Rome.* (Oxford: Oxford University Press, A.D. 2008), pp. 85–87; Pope Leo I. *Epistolae 10–14,* in *Patrologia Latina,* ed. J.-P. Migne, Vol. 54.]

Projectus was also returned to his rightful position. Meanwhile, Hilary—who had returned to Arles before the conclusion of the synod—was stripped by the pope of his jurisdiction over other Gallic provinces and of his metropolitan authority over the province of Vienne. He was permitted to retain only his own diocese of Arles.

Assertion of Roman Primacy in Gaul and Illyria

Pope Leo the Great revealed the decisions concerning his conflict with St. Hilary in a letter to the bishops of the Province of Vienne (*Epistle 10*). Alongside this letter, he enclosed an imperial edict issued by Emperor Valentinian III on July 8, A.D. 445. This decree formally endorsed the pope's disciplinary measures against St. Hilary and solemnly recognized the primacy of the Bishop of Rome over the universal Church.

Upon his return to Arles, Hilary sought reconciliation with the pope. Peace was restored between the two venerable churchmen, and after Hilary's death in A.D. 449, Leo honored him with the title *beatae memoriae* ("of blessed memory").

The Legacy of Pope Leo

When *Ravennius*[23] succeeded St. Hilary as bishop of Arles, Leo extended warm and congratulatory letters to both Ravennius and the bishops of the province (*Epistles 40 and 41*), affirming the unity of the Gallican episcopate with Rome. Not long afterward, Ravennius consecrated a bishop to succeed the late Bishop of Vaison. This act drew criticism from the Archbishop of Vienne, who happened to be in Rome at the time.

In response, the bishops of the Province of Arles jointly petitioned Leo, requesting the restoration of certain rights to Ravennius that had been stripped from his predecessor. On May 5, A.D. 450, Leo granted their appeal (*Epistle 66*). The Archbishop of Vienne was limited to oversight of only a few suffragan sees—Valence, Tarentaise, Geneva, and Grenoble—while all other dioceses in the province were placed under the jurisdiction of the Archbishop

---

[23] **Ravennius:** who succeeded St. Hilary of Arles as Bishop of Arles in A.D. 449, is noted for his conciliatory approach toward the Roman See. Unlike his predecessor, whose assertive metropolitan claims had sparked jurisdictional tensions, Ravennius sought to mend relations with Pope Leo I and align the Gallican Church more closely with Roman ecclesiastical authority. His tenure marks a pivotal shift in Arles from regional autonomy to papal cooperation, helping to stabilize the church hierarchy in Gaul.

    [Dunn, Geoffrey D. *The Bishop of Rome in Late Antiquity.* (Farnham: Ashgate, A.D. 2015), pp. 128–130; Pope Leo I. *Epistola 59*, in *Patrologia Latina*, ed. J.-P. Migne, Vol. 54.]

of Arles. Once again, Arles was confirmed as the central liaison

between the Gallican Church and the Holy See.

Leo also entrusted Ravennius with the responsibility of

disseminating his now-famous letter to *Flavian of Constantinople*[24]

concerning the doctrine of the Incarnation (*Epistle 67*). In response,

Ravennius convened a synod of forty-four bishops. In their synodal

statement of A.D. 451, the assembled bishops accepted Leo's letter as

a formal symbol of the faith (*Epistle 29*). Leo's reply further

emphasized the condemnation of the *Nestorian heresy*[25] (*Epistle 102*).

---

[24] **Flavian of Constantinople:** served as Archbishop from A.D. 446 to 449 and became a central figure in the Christological debates of the 5th-century A.D. He condemned Eutyches, a proponent of monophysitism, which triggered the convening of the Second Council of Ephesus (A.D. 449), later condemned as the *Latrocinium* or "Robber Council." There, Flavian was deposed and beaten so severely that he died from his injuries shortly thereafter. Pope Leo I wrote in Flavian's defense, most notably through his *Tome*, which articulated the doctrine of the hypostatic union and laid the foundation for Flavian's posthumous vindication at the Council of Chalcedon in A.D. 451.

> [Pope Leo I. *Epistola 28 (Tome to Flavian)*, in *Patrologia Latina*, ed. J.-P. Migne, Vol. 54; Price, Richard and Gaddis, Michael. *The Acts of the Council of Chalcedon, Vol. 1.* (Liverpool: Liverpool University Press, A.D. 2005), pp. 11–22.]

[25] **Nestorian heresy:** attributed to Nestorius, Patriarch of Constantinople (A.D. 428–431), proposed that Christ existed as two distinct persons—one human and one divine—rather than a single Person with two natures. This Christological dualism was condemned at the Council of Ephesus in A.D. 431 for fracturing the unity of Christ's person. Pope Leo I consistently rejected Nestorianism, affirming the hypostatic union in his epistolary responses to bishops in both the East and West. Nestorius's teachings sparked widespread controversy, contributing to long-term divisions in the Eastern Church.

> [McGuckin, John. *St. Cyril of Alexandria and the Christological Controversy.* (Crestwood: St. Vladimir's Seminary Press, A.D. 2004), pp. 244–248; Pope Leo I. *Epistolae 33, 35, and 124*, in *Patrologia Latina*, ed. J.-P. Migne, Vol. 54.]

The Legacy of Pope Leo

The papal vicariate of Arles maintained the elevated status that Leo had conferred upon it for many years to come. Elsewhere, Leo likewise reinforced papal authority through another vicariate— that of the bishops of Thessalonica, whose jurisdiction extended over Eastern Illyria, a region under the Eastern Roman Empire. This vicariate was specifically tasked with safeguarding the rights of the Roman See in the East.

Leo appointed *Bishop Anastasius*[26] of Thessalonica as vicar, continuing the precedent set by *Pope Siricius,*[27] who had earlier appointed *Bishop Anysius.*[28] The role came with significant

---

[26] **Bishop Anastasius:** successor of Anysius, played a significant role in advancing Roman ecclesiastical authority in Illyricum. As a bishop, he navigated complex relations with the Eastern Church, balancing local autonomy and papal oversight. Pope Leo I would later intervene in disputes surrounding Anastasius, asserting his own papal authority and reinforcing the role of the bishop of Rome as the central arbiter of ecclesiastical matters in the West.
[Meyendorff, John. *The Orthodox Church: Its Past and Its Role in the World Today.* (New York: St. Vladimir's Seminary Press, A.D. 1989), pp. 102–106; Pope Leo I, *Epistola 30*, in *Patrologia Latina*, ed. J.-P. Migne, Vol. 54.]

[27] **Pope Siricius:** (reigned A.D. 384–399), is often credited with being the first to adopt a distinctively "papal" tone in his decrees, exercising a strong centralizing influence within the church. His decretals, issued with universal authority, established important precedents for papal governance. Siricius's appointment of Anysius as vicar in Illyricum demonstrated his commitment to Roman primacy, a vision that would be fully realized under his successor, Pope Leo I.
[Anson, Peter F. *The Pope's Servants: A History of the Papal Household.* (London: Burns & Oates, A.D. 1967), pp. 55–58.]

[28] **Bishop Anysius:** appointed by Pope Siricius as his representative in Illyricum, set an important precedent for the papal vicar institution that would later be used by Pope Leo I to assert Roman influence in remote regions. Anysius's role as a papal delegate in the eastern provinces exemplified the increasing centralization of papal authority, a strategy that Leo would adopt and refine. Leo would frequently

responsibility: the vicar was to consecrate metropolitan bishops, convene synods with all bishops of Eastern Illyria, and supervise their governance. However, matters of major importance were still to be referred directly to Rome (*Epistles 5, 6, and 8*).

Unfortunately, Anastasius exercised his powers in an overly autocratic and oppressive manner. In response, Leo rebuked him sharply and issued more detailed instructions to curb his excessive use of authority (*Epistle 14*).

Guardian of Discipline

In Pope Leo the Great's understanding of his role as the Church's supreme pastor, the rigorous preservation of ecclesiastical discipline held a central place. Amid the chaos brought on by the *barbarian invasions*[29]—disrupting civil order and eroding moral

---

invoke such earlier papal interventions in Illyricum, including those of Anysius, to support his own claims to universal ecclesiastical supremacy.

    [Krautheimer, Richard. *Papal Architecture in the Early Middle Ages.* (New York: Oxford University Press, A.D. 1983), pp. 67–70.]

[29] **"Barbarian invasions"** commonly refers to the large-scale migrations and military incursions by various Germanic tribes—such as the Visigoths, Vandals, Ostrogoths, and others—into the Western Roman Empire during the 4th- and 5th-centuries A.D. These invasions weakened the Roman state's infrastructure and contributed to the eventual fall of the Western Roman Empire. The deposition of the last Roman emperor, Romulus Augustulus, by the Germanic leader Odoacer in A.D. 476 is traditionally viewed as the formal end of the Western Empire, although the collapse had been a gradual process.

    [Heather, Peter. *The Fall of the Roman Empire: A New History of Rome and the Barbarians.* (Oxford: Oxford University Press, A.D. 2005), pp. 95–100.]

norms—Leo saw firm governance of the Church as not only necessary but urgent.

With tireless dedication, he enforced strict adherence to canonical norms and was unafraid to issue correction when discipline faltered. His letters on these matters were wide-ranging, directed to bishops across the Western Empire. Italian bishops received repeated exhortations to uphold discipline (*Epistles 4, 19, 166, and 168*), while those in Sicily were admonished for liturgical deviations, particularly regarding the rites of Baptism (*Epistle 16*). Another letter addressed broader concerns of ecclesiastical conduct in the region (*Epistle 17*).

A particularly weighty disciplinary ruling was delivered to *Bishop Rusticus*[30] of Narbonne (*Epistle 167*), reflecting Leo's insistence that pastoral responsibility be met with moral clarity and organizational order.

In North Africa, the situation was even more dire. The Vandal conquest had plunged the Church there into turmoil. To

---

[30] **Bishop Rusticus:** was a 5th-century A.D. bishop who received a disciplinary ruling from Pope Leo I as part of the papal efforts to maintain doctrinal purity and pastoral responsibility. Narbonne, located in southern France near the Mediterranean coast, was an important city during the late Roman Empire and the early medieval period.

[Moorhead, John. *Pope Leo I and the Early Church.* (Cambridge: Cambridge University Press, A.D. 1999), pp. 87–90; Pope Leo I, *Epistola 59*, in *Patrologia Latina*, ed. J.-P. Migne, Vol. 54.]

assess the damage and bring clarity, Leo dispatched the Roman priest

Potentius[31] to gather an account. Based on his report, Leo composed a

detailed letter addressing the province's bishops, offering guidance on

a wide range of ecclesiastical and disciplinary challenges (*Epistle 12*).

Leo also turned his attention eastward. On July 21, A.D. 445,

he wrote to *Dioscorus of Alexandria,*[32] urging strict fidelity to the canons

and practices of the Roman Church (*Epistle 9*). Through such

interventions, the primacy of the Roman See was demonstrated in

manifold and unmistakable ways.

---

[31] **Potentius:** was an important cleric in the 5th-century A.D. who was tasked with reporting on ecclesiastical matters in the regions under his oversight. His report, which prompted Pope Leo I's *Epistle 12*, exemplifies Leo's active engagement in resolving doctrinal and disciplinary issues within the Christian Church. Potentius's role was crucial not only in gathering information but also in representing the Roman papacy's interest in enforcing uniformity in the provinces. His correspondence with Leo helped solidify the papacy's role as an authoritative figure in managing ecclesiastical matters across the empire.
> [Price, Richard. *The Acts of the Council of Chalcedon.* (Liverpool: Liverpool University Press, A.D. 2005), pp. 101–105; Pope Leo I, *Epistola 12*, in *Patrologia Latina*, ed. J.-P. Migne, Vol. 54.]

[32] **Dioscorus of Alexandria:** was the Patriarch of Alexandria during a period marked by both theological controversy and political turbulence. His tenure, particularly his involvement in the Robber Council of Ephesus (A.D. 449), made him a contentious figure within the broader Christian community. While Pope Leo I urged him to adhere to the Roman Church's canons and practices in his *Epistle 9*, Dioscorus's actions often contrasted sharply with Leo's views on the nature of Christ and the importance of theological orthodoxy. His eventual deposition at the Council of Chalcedon (A.D. 451) underlined the tension between Alexandria and Rome, with Leo championing the Roman See's role in defining Christological doctrine.
> [Norris Jr., Richard A. *The Christological Controversy.* (Fortress Press, A.D. 1980), pp. 75–78; Pope Leo I, *Epistola 9*, in *Patrologia Latina*, ed. J.-P. Migne, Vol. 54.]

The Legacy of Pope Leo

Yet it was in the midst of the Christological controversies rocking the Eastern Church that Leo's leadership shone most brightly. His deep learning, pastoral resolve, and intellectual clarity positioned him as the central figure navigating the storm. From his first intervention—his letter to *Eutyches*[33] on June 1, A.D. 448 (*Epistle 20*)—to his final correspondence with the newly installed orthodox Patriarch of Alexandria, *Timotheus Salophaciolus,*[34] on August 18, A.D. 460 (*Epistle 171*), Leo's engagement was methodical, confident, and rooted in his understanding of the Petrine office.

---

[33] **Eutyches:** was a 5th-century A.D. monk and theologian who became the focal point of a significant Christological controversy. He was accused of heresy for advocating a form of Monophysitism, which held that Christ had only one nature, divine rather than both human and divine. Pope Leo I's intervention, in his letter to Eutyches (*Epistle 20*), was pivotal in condemning this view, reaffirming the orthodox position on the dual nature of Christ. Leo's theological stance laid the foundation for the subsequent decisions at the Council of Chalcedon (A.D. 451).

> [Norris Jr., Richard A. *The Christological Controversy.* (Fortress Press, A.D. 1980), pp. 75–78; Pope Leo I, *Epistola 20*, in *Patrologia Latina*, ed. J.-P. Migne, Vol. 54.]

[34] **Timotheus Salophaciolus:** installed as Patriarch of Alexandria in A.D. 451 after the deposition of Dioscorus, became an important figure in the post-Chalcedonian Church. His appointment was supported by Pope Leo I, who, through his correspondence (*Epistle 171*), reinforced his authority in Alexandria and ensured loyalty to the decisions made at Chalcedon regarding the nature of Christ. Timotheus's leadership marked a critical period of transition in Alexandria, where the theological disputes that had marked the previous decades began to subside.

> [Meyendorff, John. *Imperial Unity and Christian Divisions: The Church 450–680 A.D.* (St. Vladimir's Seminary Press, A.D. 1989), pp. 142–145; Pope Leo I, *Epistola 171*, in *Patrologia Latina*, ed. J.-P. Migne, Vol. 54.]

Through these efforts, he not only upheld doctrinal integrity but also modeled a courageous and principled defense of the faith in one of the Church's most turbulent ages.

The Christological Crisis

When Eutyches, a proponent of Monophysitism, was excommunicated by Flavian, Patriarch of Constantinople, he turned to Pope Leo I for support. Leo, after a careful examination of the theological controversy, responded with one of the most important documents in Christological history—his majestic *Tome to Flavian* (*Epistle 28*). In it, he clearly and powerfully affirmed the doctrine of the Incarnation: that in the one Person of Christ, the divine and human natures are united without confusion or division.

The following year, in A.D. 449, a synod was convened in Ephesus—later condemned by Leo as the "Robber Synod" due to its disorder and coercion. The council not only overturned Flavian's decisions but subjected him and other orthodox bishops to violent treatment. In the wake of this crisis, Flavian and other Eastern prelates appealed urgently to Leo, who responded by dispatching a series of forceful letters to Constantinople. He addressed *Emperor*

Theodosius II[35] and *Empress Pulcheria,*[36] imploring them to call a legitimate general council to restore unity and doctrinal clarity to the Church.

Leo also enlisted the support of the Western imperial court— Emperor Valentinian III and his influential mother, Galla Placidia— particularly during their visit to Rome in A.D. 450. His efforts bore fruit the next year, when a general council was held in Chalcedon under the new emperor, *Marcian.*[37]

---

[35] **Emperor Theodosius II:** (reigned A.D. 408–450), presided over a critical period in the development of Christian doctrine, particularly through his role in convening the Second Council of Ephesus in A.D. 449. Prompted by appeals from Dioscorus of Alexandria and others, Theodosius authorized the gathering, which controversially reinstated Eutyches and condemned Flavian of Constantinople. Though intended to restore unity, the council instead provoked widespread backlash and was later labeled the *Latrocinium* or "Robber Council." Theodosius's deference to ecclesiastical factions and court influence, especially from figures like the eunuch Chrysaphius, ultimately weakened imperial authority in theological arbitration.
    [Price, Richard and Gaddis, Michael. *The Acts of the Council of Chalcedon, Vol. 1.* (Liverpool: Liverpool University Press, A.D. 2005), pp. 7–14.]

[36] **Empress Pulcheria:** (A.D. 399–453), sister of Theodosius II, played a formative role in shaping imperial religious policy throughout the first half of the 5th-century A.D. A staunch advocate of Nicene orthodoxy and reverence for the Virgin Mary, Pulcheria served as regent and later co-ruler, wielding considerable influence even while out of formal power during her brother's reign. After Theodosius's death in A.D. 450, she returned to prominence, orchestrating the ascension of Marcian as emperor and overseeing the theological settlement at the Council of Chalcedon (A.D. 451), which affirmed the dyophysite position articulated in Pope Leo I's *Tome.* Her patronage of orthodoxy and assertive ecclesiastical diplomacy made her one of the most influential imperial women in early church history.
    [McGuckin, John. *Saint Cyril of Alexandria and the Christological Controversy.* (Crestwood: St. Vladimir's Seminary Press, A.D. 2004), pp. 231–235.]

[37] **Emperor Marcian:** (reigned A.D. 450–457), played a pivotal role in shaping the post-Theodosian theological and political landscape of the Eastern Roman Empire. A staunch supporter of Chalcedonian orthodoxy, Marcian convened the Council of

Pope Leo I

At Chalcedon in A.D. 451, Leo's *Tome* was read aloud and received with universal acclaim, recognized as an authoritative declaration of the Catholic faith on the mystery of Christ's two natures. The Council's doctrinal decrees, rooted in Leo's letter, were approved by the pope, though he rejected one particular canon that sought to elevate the see of Constantinople at the expense of the traditional Eastern patriarchates.

On March 21, A.D. 453, Leo issued a circular letter (*Epistle 114*) reaffirming his Christological definition, sealing its place as doctrinal bedrock. Meanwhile, through the diplomatic work of *Bishop Julian of Cos,*[38] Leo's legate in Constantinople, he continued to

---

Chalcedon in A.D. 451 to address the Christological controversies inflamed by the Second Council of Ephesus (the so-called "Robber Council" of A.D. 449). His endorsement of Pope Leo I's Tome and his backing of the Council's decrees marked a decisive imperial affirmation of the doctrine of Christ's two natures, divine and human. Marcian's reign provided the political stability necessary for the formalization and enforcement of Chalcedonian doctrine across the empire.
  [Bowman, Steven B. *The Jews of Byzantium.* (Cambridge University Press, A.D. 1985), pp. 25–28.]

[38] **Bishop Julian of Cos:** served as one of Pope Leo I's most trusted diplomatic agents and played a crucial role in maintaining Roman influence in the Eastern Church after Chalcedon. As Leo's legate in Constantinople, Julian worked to secure imperial support for Chalcedonian orthodoxy and to counterbalance attempts by the see of Constantinople to assert primacy over the older patriarchates. His efforts helped preserve the doctrinal integrity of the Chalcedonian settlement and ensure continued Eastern respect for Roman theological authority. Julian's tact and loyalty were essential in the fraught post-conciliar period when ecclesial politics and imperial policy were deeply intertwined.
  [Demacopoulos, George E. *The Invention of Peter: Apostolic Discourse and Papal Authority in Late Antiquity.* (University of Pennsylvania Press, A.D. 2013), pp. 96–99.]

safeguard the Church's interests in the East. He successfully

persuaded the new Eastern Emperor, Leo I, to depose the heretical

and irregular patriarch, Timotheus Ailurus, from the Alexandrian See.

In his place, a faithful and orthodox bishop—Timotheus

Salophaciolus—was installed, receiving Leo's blessing in what would

become the pope's final letter to the Eastern Church. Through these

decisive interventions, Leo not only defended the integrity of

Christian doctrine but preserved the unity of the Church in a time of

doctrinal peril and imperial tension.

Defender of Rome

While Pope Leo I exercised broad pastoral authority over the

Church across East and West, he never lost sight of the spiritual and

temporal needs of his own flock in Rome. His leadership during

moments of profound crisis elevated him not only as a spiritual

father but also as a protector of the city itself.

In A.D. 452, when Northern Italy lay ravaged by the advance

of *Attila the Hun,*[39] it was Leo who stood between Rome and

---

[39] **Attila the Hun:** ruler of the Hunnic Empire from A.D. 434–453, was one of the most feared enemies of the Roman world. In A.D. 452, after ravaging the northern Italian cities of Aquileia, Milan, and others, he advanced toward Rome. According to later accounts, Pope Leo I, accompanied by Roman officials, met Attila near the

destruction. At the request of Emperor Valentinian III, Leo traveled

north with *Consul Avienus[40]* and *Prefect Trigetius[41]* to meet Attila at the

River Mincio, near Mantua. In that historic encounter, the pope's

commanding moral presence and persuasive authority moved the

fearsome warlord to abandon his plans of attacking Rome and

instead pursue peace with the Empire.

Just three years later, Rome again faced danger—this time

from the Vandals under *King Genseric.[42]* The city fell in A.D. 455 and

---

River Mincio. While the exact cause of Attila's retreat remains debated—some
credit disease, famine, or military pressure—Christian tradition emphasizes Leo's
personal influence and divine protection.
> [Kelly, Christopher. *Attila the Hun: Barbarian Terror and the Fall of the Roman
> Empire.* (Random House, A.D. 2009), pp. 198–204.]

[40] **Consul Avienus:** a Roman aristocrat and member of the senatorial elite, served
as consul in A.D. 450 and played a key diplomatic role during the mid-5th-century
A.D. He was one of the envoys chosen by Emperor Valentinian III to accompany
Pope Leo I in the delegation that met Attila the Hun. Though little is recorded
about his direct role in the negotiations, his selection suggests high political trust
and standing. His participation alongside Leo underscored the coordination
between imperial and ecclesiastical authority during times of crisis.
> [Bury, J.B. *History of the Later Roman Empire, Vol. 1.* (Macmillan, A.D.
> 1923), pp. 307–309.]

[41] **Prefect Trigetius:** the Praetorian Prefect of Italy, was a senior administrative
official under Emperor Valentinian III. He joined Pope Leo I and Consul Avienus
on the mission to negotiate with Attila in A.D. 452. His inclusion in the delegation
reflected the seriousness of the threat and the need to unite both religious and civil
authorities in defense of Rome. While Trigetius remains a relatively obscure figure,
his role in this diplomatic episode highlights the interplay between Roman
bureaucracy and ecclesiastical leadership.
> [Oost, Stewart. *Galla Placidia Augusta: A Biographical Essay.* (University of
> Chicago Press, A.D. 1968), pp. 368–370.]

[42] **King Genseric:** king of the Vandals and Alans (reigned A.D. 428–477), led his
people from Hispania to North Africa, establishing a powerful kingdom centered in
Carthage. In A.D. 455, following the assassination of Emperor Valentinian III and
an invitation from the Empress Licinia Eudoxia, Genseric invaded Italy and sacked

was subjected to two weeks of plunder. Yet Leo, intervening once

more, secured Genseric's promise that the lives of the inhabitants

would be spared and the city's buildings preserved from wanton

destruction. These extraordinary acts of diplomacy demonstrated the

immense moral authority Leo wielded, even in the volatile realm of

imperial politics and warfare.

Leo maintained close and respectful ties with the Western

imperial court. In A.D. 450, Emperor Valentinian III, accompanied

by *Empress Eudoxia*[43] and his mother *Galla Placidia*,[44] visited Rome. On

---

Rome. Pope Leo I met him at the city gates and famously persuaded him to spare the inhabitants and refrain from burning the city. While the Vandals looted Rome for two weeks, Leo's intervention likely mitigated the destruction.

[Merrills & Miles. *The Vandals*. (Blackwell Publishing, A.D. 2010), pp. 92–96.]

[43] **Empress Eudoxia:** was the daughter of Theodosius II and wife of Western Emperor Valentinian III. As a member of the Theodosian dynasty, she embodied the imperial alliance between East and West. After her husband's assassination in A.D. 455, she was reportedly forced to marry his successor Petronius Maximus and may have appealed to the Vandal king Genseric for help—an action that possibly precipitated the Vandal sack of Rome. Eudoxia's earlier visit to Rome in A.D. 450 alongside Valentinian III reflected the imperial court's efforts to publicly align itself with the papacy, particularly during Pope Leo I's rise in moral and doctrinal authority.

[Sivan, Hagith. *Galla Placidia: The Last Roman Empress*. (Oxford University Press, A.D. 2011), pp. 235–237.]

[44] **Galla Placidia:** (A.D. 388–450), daughter of Emperor Theodosius I and mother of Emperor Valentinian III, played a pivotal political role during the early-5th-century A.D. As regent for her young son, she exercised effective control over the Western Roman Empire from A.D. 425 until his majority. A devout Christian, Galla Placidia was a significant patron of the Church and maintained strong ties with several bishops, including Leo I. Her influence helped secure the stability of the Western court and laid the groundwork for Leo's collaboration with imperial authority. Her visit to Rome in A.D. 450, near the end of her life, symbolized the enduring alliance between Church and imperial power.

---

the Feast of the Chair of St. Peter, February 22, the imperial family, attended by a dazzling retinue, participated in the solemn liturgy at St. Peter's Basilica, where Leo delivered a sermon of striking eloquence and spiritual force.

Preserver of Beauty

Beyond his political and pastoral efforts, Leo left a lasting legacy through his contributions to the sacred architecture of Rome. He oversaw the restoration of several churches and personally undertook building projects to honor the martyrs and beautify the city's Christian heritage. He constructed a basilica over the tomb of *Pope Cornelius*[45] along *the Via Appia*[46] and replaced the roof of St. Paul

---

[Oost, Stewart. *Galla Placidia Augusta: A Biographical Essay.* (University of Chicago Press, A.D. 1968), pp. 260–265.]

[45] **Pope Cornelius:** (A.D. 251–253), was elected during the persecution of Christians under Emperor Decius. He defended the Church's authority during the Novatianist schism and upheld the reintegration of lapsed Christians after persecution. Martyred during the reign of Gallus, Cornelius was buried in the Catacomb of Callixtus along the Via Appia. Pope Leo I's decision to construct a basilica over Cornelius's tomb signified both a reverence for early Christian martyrs and a conscious effort to physically embed the memory of papal continuity into the Roman landscape.

[Kelly, J.N.D. *The Oxford Dictionary of Popes.* (Oxford University Press, A.D. 1986), p. 20.]

[46] **The Via Appia:** ("Appian Way"), was one of the oldest and most strategically significant Roman roads, begun in B.C. 312. It connected Rome to southern Italy and became a favored burial route for Christians during periods of persecution. Numerous catacombs and shrines—including those of Saints Sebastian, Callixtus, and Cornelius—line the road. By the 5th-century A.D., papal construction along the

Outside the Walls after it had been destroyed by lightning, initiating

further improvements to the structure. The magnificent mosaic on *the*

Arch of Triumph,[47] which still survives today, was commissioned by

Empress Galla Placidia at Leo's urging.

He also restored and enhanced St. Peter's Basilica on the

Vatican Hill. During his pontificate, a devout Roman noblewoman

named Demetria erected a church in honor of St. Stephen on her

estate along the Via Appia—a basilica whose ruins have since been

excavated.

In all these works—diplomatic, pastoral, and architectural—

Leo the Great revealed the full stature of a man who was both

---

Via Appia symbolized both pilgrimage devotion and Rome's transformation from
imperial to Christian capital.

> [Krautheimer, Richard. *Rome: Profile of a City, 312–1308.* (Princeton
> University Press, A.D. 1980), pp. 42–44.]

[47] **The Arch of Triumph:** (or *Triumphal Arch*), in the Basilica of St. Paul Outside
the Walls is crowned by a stunning 5th-century A.D. mosaic depicting Christ
between the apostles Peter and Paul. According to tradition and some
archaeological evidence, this mosaic was commissioned by Empress Galla Placidia
at the behest of Pope Leo I, reflecting both the imperial family's investment in
Rome's Christian monuments and Leo's commitment to doctrinal clarity through
sacred art. The arch served as a visual catechesis of Christological orthodoxy amid
the controversies of the era.

> [Brenk, Beat. *The Apse, the Image and the Icon: An Historical Perspective of the
> Apse as a Space for Images.* (Dumbarton Oaks Papers, A.D. 1987), pp. 13–
> 14.]

shepherd and statesman, a guardian of doctrine and defender of civilization.

Voice of Rome and Doctor of the Church

Pope Leo I was as tireless in the spiritual formation of his people as he was in defending their peace. His sermons—of which ninety-six authentic examples have been preserved—are monuments of theological depth, clarity of expression, and lofty rhetorical style. Among them, the first five, delivered annually on the anniversary of his consecration, reveal his profound sense of the sacred dignity of the papal office and his unwavering belief in the primacy of the Bishop of Rome. This conviction was not abstract—it shaped every aspect of his ministry as the Church's supreme pastor.

Leo's legacy extends beyond the spoken word. His correspondence—143 surviving letters, along with 30 addressed to him—forms a vital part of the historical record of the Church in the 5th-century A.D. These letters document a bishop deeply engaged with the theological, political, and pastoral challenges of his time, and provide invaluable insight into the life of the early Church.

The Legacy of Pope Leo

Though not directly compiled by Leo himself, the *Sacramentarium Leonianum*—a liturgical book of orations and Mass prefaces from the 6ᵗʰ-century A.D.—bears his name and reflects the enduring spiritual influence of his pontificate. His thought and tone resounded so powerfully that even generations later, they would still shape the Church's prayer.

Pope Leo I died on November 10, A.D. 461, and was first buried in the vestibule of St. Peter's Basilica. More than two centuries later, in A.D. 688, Pope Sergius I had his remains transferred into the basilica itself, enshrining them beneath an altar dedicated in his honor. Today, his relics rest beneath the Altar of St. Leo in St. Peter's, where pilgrims still venerate the memory of a pontiff who embodied both theological wisdom and pastoral strength.

In A.D. 1754, Pope Benedict XIV formally recognized Leo's enduring contribution to the Church by declaring him a *Doctor of the Church*.[48] His feast is celebrated on April 11 in the Latin Church, and

---

[48] **"Doctor of the Church"** (*doctor ecclesiæ*), is a formal title bestowed by the Catholic Church on certain saints recognized for their eminent learning and significant contribution to theology or doctrine. The designation, first officially used in the medieval period, signifies both orthodoxy of teaching and universal relevance. While early figures such as Augustine of Hippo, Gregory the Great, Jerome, and Ambrose were venerated informally as Doctors, the title became more systematically applied by the papacy in later centuries.

on February 18 in the Eastern tradition, affirming his universal legacy.

Pope Leo the Great stands as a timeless witness to the unity of truth and love—a bishop whose voice echoed with apostolic authority and whose heart beat with pastoral devotion.

[Pope Benedict XVI. *Great Christian Thinkers: From the Early Church Through the Middle Ages.* (San Francisco: Ignatius Press, A.D. 2011), pp. 13–17.]

Chapter II

Pope Leo II (A.D. 682-683)

The Delayed Consecration

In the wake of fierce theological storms and imperial

tensions, the brief but potent pontificate of Pope Leo II, who reigned

as Pope from A.D. 682 until 683, emerged as a clarifying light,

bridging the deep intellectual piety of his predecessor *St. Agatho*[49] and

the enduring need for orthodoxy and unity in the Church. Though

---

[49] **St. Agatho:** served as Pope from A.D. 678 to 681 and played a pivotal role in the Sixth Ecumenical Council, also known as the Third Council of Constantinople. Agatho's firm stance on the condemnation of Monothelitism—teaching that Christ had two wills, one divine and one human—helped to clarify and solidify the Church's position on Christological doctrine. His role in ensuring the success of the council, despite the political pressure from Byzantine emperors, underscored his commitment to the orthodoxy of the faith. Agatho's involvement in the council marked a critical moment in the history of the Church, as it established a clear distinction between orthodoxy and heresy in the East and West.

[Meyendorff, John. *Imperial Unity and Christian Divisions: The Church 450–680 A.D.* (St. Vladimir's Seminary Press, A.D. 1989), pp. 150-155.]

his reign was short—less than a year—it was a time rich in doctrinal finality, liturgical refinement, and institutional negotiation.

Born in Sicily as Leo, son of Paul, the future pope ascended to the See of Peter not in triumph but through the slow machinery of imperial bureaucracy. Though elected in A.D. 681, his consecration was delayed for over a year—an emblem of the lingering Byzantine influence over Rome, where papal confirmations still required imperial assent.

St. Agatho had died in early January of A.D. 681, and Leo was elected shortly thereafter. Yet his formal consecration did not occur until August 17, A.D. 682—seventeen long months later. The delay stemmed from the evolving relationship between the Holy See and *Emperor Constantine IV Pogonatus.*[50]

---

[50] **Emperor Constantine IV Pogonatus:** (reigned A.D. 668-685), is is best known for his leadership during the Third Council of Constantinople (A.D. 681), where the Monothelite heresy was formally condemned. Constantine IV's decision to call the council was motivated by both theological concerns and political pressures, as the Byzantine Empire sought to address divisions within its Christian population. His support for Pope Agatho's theological stance on the two wills of Christ helped pave the way for the doctrinal resolution that solidified the Eastern and Western Churches' positions on Christological issues. His reign was crucial in bridging the gap between East and West in doctrinal matters, even though tensions remained between the papacy and the Byzantine Empire.

[Jones, A.H.M. *The Later Roman Empire.* (Harvard University Press, A.D. 1964), pp. 774-778.]

For nearly a century, each newly elected pope had to pay a tax to the imperial treasury before receiving confirmation from the emperor. St. Agatho had begun discussions to abolish or lessen this humiliating practice, and Leo inherited both the negotiations and the limbo they created. The emperor's hesitation to finalize Leo's confirmation likely stemmed from these very talks, revealing the delicate balance between ecclesiastical independence and imperial oversight.

Despite the delay, Leo took up his office with scholarly energy and ecclesial conviction. The challenges that awaited him were not new, but they required a steady and intellectually forceful hand.

The Sixth Ecumenical Council

Leo's pontificate is most notable for his ratification and dissemination of the decrees of the Third Council of Constantinople (A.D. 680–681), also known as the Sixth Ecumenical Council. Convened to resolve the controversy of *Monothelitism*[51]—the belief

---

[51] **Monothelitism:** a Christological heresy that emerged in the 7th-century A.D., posited that Christ had only one will—the divine will—rather than two distinct wills, one divine and one human, as defined by orthodox Christian doctrine. This teaching was initially promoted by the Byzantine Emperor Heraclius and his patriarch, Sergius I of Constantinople, as a means to reconcile theological disputes between the Eastern and Western Church. However, Monothelitism was formally

that Christ had two natures but only one will—the council

condemned the heresy as incompatible with the full humanity and

divinity of Christ. The Council had been presided over by the legates

of Pope Agatho, and its decisions had theological and ecclesiastical

consequences for East and West alike.

Upon receiving the acts of the council, Leo took the

extraordinary step of translating key parts from Greek into Latin so

that the teachings could be fully understood and adopted throughout

the Western Church. This act was more than clerical housekeeping; it

symbolized the pope's commitment to doctrinal clarity and ecclesial

unity.

In confirming the council's decrees, Leo explicitly recognized

their fidelity to the apostolic tradition. "The holy and universal sixth

synod," he wrote in the letter, "has followed in all things the teaching

of the Apostles and approved Fathers… and by the authority of

blessed Peter do confirm them."[52] In these words, Leo anchored the

---

condemned at the Third Council of Constantinople (A.D. 681), which affirmed the doctrine of Dyothelitism, the belief that Christ possessed both a divine and human will, in accordance with the Nicene Creed.
[Norris Jr., Richard A. *The Christological Controversy*. (Fortress Press, A.D. 1980), pp. 75-78.]
[52] Pope Leo II. *Epistola 2*. In *Patrologia Latina*, Vol. 87, edited by *J.-P. Migne,* cols. 855–856.

council's authority in the Roman See itself, reinforcing the belief—

expressed clearly by St. Agatho—that the Church of Rome, protected

by the promise of Christ to Peter, could not err in faith.

The Condemnation of Pope Honorius

Perhaps most controversial was Leo's confirmation of the

council's condemnation of his predecessor, Pope Honorius I.

Honorius had not promulgated heresy outright, but his failure to

condemn Monothelitism left him vulnerable to posthumous rebuke.

Leo, navigating the tension between papal authority and

accountability, nuanced the condemnation.

He did not accuse Honorius of teaching heresy, but of failing

in his duty: "Honorius... did not attempt to sanctify this Apostolic

Church with the teaching of Apostolic tradition, but by profane

treachery permitted its purity to be polluted."[53] This condemnation—

measured, theologically precise, and politically courageous—became

a key point of reference in later debates over papal infallibility. It was

recited in subsequent councils, including Nicaea II (A.D. 787) and

Constantinople IV (A.D. 869), and became part of the oath sworn by

---

[53] Ibid.

popes for centuries thereafter. In accordance with the papal mandate, a synod was held at Toledo in A.D. 684 in which the Council of Constantinople was accepted, demonstrating Leo's effort to ensure the doctrinal clarity of the West aligned with the conciliar decrees.

"My predecessor, Pope Agatho of Apostolic memory, together with his honorable Synod, preached this norm of the right apostolic tradition. This he sent by letter to your piety by his own legates, demonstrating it and confirming it by the usage of the holy and approved teachers of the Church. And now the holy and great Synod, celebrated by the favor of God and your own has accepted it and embraced it in all things with us, as recognizing in it the pure teaching of the blessed Peter, the prince of the Apostles, and discovering in it the marks of sound piety. Therefore the holy and universal sixth synod, which by the will of God your clemency summoned and presided, has followed in all things the teaching of the Apostles and approved Fathers. And because, as we have said, it has perfectly preached the definition of the true faith which the Apostolic See of blessed Peter the Apostle (whose office we unworthily hold) also reverently receives, therefore we, and by our ministry this reverend Apostolic See, wholly and with full agreement do consent to the definitions made by it, and by the authority of

blessed Peter do confirm them, even as we have received firmness

from the Lord Himself upon the firm rock which is Christ…"

"And in like manner we anathematize the inventors of the new error,

that is, Theodore, Bishop of Pharan, Sergius, Pyrrhus, Paul and Peter,

betrayers rather than leaders of the Church of Constantinople, and

also Honorius, who did not attempt to sanctify this Apostolic Church

with the teaching of Apostolic tradition, but by profane treachery

permitted its purity to be polluted"[54]

The Ravenna Dispute: Autocephaly Contested

Pope Leo's diplomatic abilities were also tested in his dealings

with the see of Ravenna. Ravenna, long the seat of imperial authority

in Italy, had become ambitious. Its archbishops sought patriarchal

---

[54] Ibid.

privileges and independence from Rome, and in A.D. 666, *Emperor*

Constans II[55] had granted them a form of *autocephaly*.[56]

Leo moved swiftly to reverse this. He secured from

Constantine IV a revocation of the edict, thereby restoring Ravenna

to papal jurisdiction. Yet, in a move that revealed both his prudence

and his understanding of the Church's human element, Leo granted

certain concessions: he abolished the tax Ravenna's archbishops paid

upon receiving the *pallium*[57] and shortened their required stay in

Rome. While he demanded their presence in Rome for consecration,

---

[55] **Emperor Constans II:** (reigned A.D. 641–668), was the Byzantine emperor who issued the *Typos* in A.D. 648, an edict that forbade all discussion of the number of wills in Christ, in an attempt to suppress the growing controversy over Monothelitism. His policy of enforced silence alienated both Eastern and Western bishops, including Pope Martin I, whom he had arrested and exiled. Constans's aggressive interference in ecclesiastical matters exemplified the ongoing tensions between imperial authority and papal independence.

> [Brooks, E.W. *Constans II and the Exarchate of Ravenna. The English Historical Review, Vol. 18, no. 72*. (A.D. 1903), pp. 625–636.]

[56] **Autocephaly:** (from the Greek *autokephalos*, meaning "self-headed"), refers to a church's independence in governance, particularly its right to elect its own primate without external approval. In late antiquity and the early medieval period, debates over autocephaly—especially concerning the privileges of the Patriarchates and regional metropolitans—often intersected with wider theological and political disputes. Rome traditionally opposed unilateral declarations of autocephaly that undermined its claim to universal jurisdiction.

> [Dvornik, Francis. *Byzantium and the Roman Primacy*. (Fordham University Press, A.D. 1966), pp. 71–75.]

[57] **Pallium:** is a liturgical vestment worn by metropolitan archbishops as a symbol of their authority and communion with the Holy See. In Late Antiquity, it also carried juridical significance, with its reception marking papal approval of a bishop's jurisdiction.

> [Noble, Thomas F. X. *The Republic of St. Peter: The Birth of the Papal State, 680–825*. (University of Pennsylvania Press, A.D. 1984), pp. 54–56.]

he allowed them to send annual emissaries in their stead thereafter. It was a masterclass in balancing authority with concession.

A Scholar, Psalmist, and Builder

Though his reign was marked by serious theological and political decisions, Leo II was not merely a statesman. According to the *Liber Pontificalis*, he was "a man of great eloquence, competently versed in Holy Scripture, proficient in Greek and Latin, and distinguished for his chanting and psalmody."[58] This musical and scriptural brilliance found expression in his promotion of liturgical music. He refined the Roman chant and contributed to the beautification of the Church's worship—his love for sacred song mirrored his devotion to doctrinal harmony.

Fearing renewed Lombard incursions into the sacred catacombs, Leo also took steps to protect Rome's most holy relics. He relocated the remains of many martyrs into a church he commissioned specifically to safeguard them. In this, Leo revealed a

---

[58] *Liber Pontificalis, ed. Louis Duchesne, 2nd ed.* (Paris: Imprimerie Nationale, A.D. 1955), p. 292.

deep reverence for tradition—not as fossilized memory but as living faith.

Death and Legacy

Pope Leo II died on July 3, A.D. 683, less than a year after his consecration. Though his reign was brief, it was marked by clarity, conciliation, and confidence in the mission of the Apostolic See. He was buried in St. Peter's Basilica, and his name entered the *Roman Martyrology*[59] as a saint, remembered on the anniversary of his death.

Leo's importance lies not only in what he did but in how he did it: with a mind trained in the Scriptures, a voice trained in the Psalms, and a will attuned to the unity of the Church. He confirmed the faith not by innovation, but by fidelity—to Peter, to Christ, and to the sound teaching that the Church had always held.

---

[59] **Roman Martyrology:** is the official liturgical book of the Roman Catholic Church, listing the names of saints, martyrs, and other holy individuals, along with the dates of their feast days. It serves as a record of those individuals recognized for their sanctity and includes both ancient and modern saints. The *Martyrology* is updated annually by the Vatican and is used for the celebration of the saints in the Roman Rite.

[*Roman Martyrology, trans. by Rev. William J. Gibbons.* (New York: Catholic Book Publishing, A.D. 1961), p. 1.]

Chapter III

Pope Leo III (A.D. 795-816)

Favor of the Franks

Pope Leo III, born Leo in Rome as the son of Atyuppius and Elizabeth, ascended to the papacy with remarkable swiftness—elected on 26 December, A.D. 795, the very day his predecessor was laid to rest, and consecrated the following day. This unusual haste may have reflected the Roman clergy's desire to secure the freedom of their election before any intervention from the powerful Frankish court. At the time of his elevation, Leo served as Cardinal-Priest of St. Susanna, located on the Quirinal Hill in Rome, and likely held the office of *vestiarius*, chief of the papal treasury and wardrobe.

Pope Leo III

Eager to secure ties with *Charlemagne*,[60] Leo sent the newly crowned Frankish king a letter announcing his unanimous election, accompanied by the keys to the confession of St. Peter and the standard of the city of Rome—symbols of honor and submission. In doing so, Leo affirmed his view of Charlemagne as the earthly protector of the Holy See. Charlemagne responded warmly, sending letters of congratulations and a generous share of the treasure seized in his victorious campaign against *the Avars*.[61] This sudden influx of wealth allowed Leo to become a notable patron of Rome, strengthening its churches and extending generous support to the city's charitable institutions.

---

[60] **Charlemagne:** also known as Charles the Great, was the King of the Franks from A.D. 768 and Emperor of the Holy Roman Empire from A.D. 800 until his death in A.D. 814. He is often credited with uniting much of Western Europe for the first time since the fall of the Roman Empire. His reign marked a significant period of cultural revival, known as the Carolingian Renaissance, and he played a key role in the spread of Christianity across Europe.
[Fried, Johannes. *Charlemagne*. (Cambridge: Polity Press, A.D. 2009), pp. 25-26.]

[61] **The Avars:** were a nomadic group originating from Central Asia, who established a significant empire in Eastern Europe during the 6th- to 9th-centuries A.D. They ruled over parts of what is now Hungary, Austria, and the Balkans. Known for their military prowess, the Avars played a key role in the early medieval period, interacting with the Byzantine Empire, the Franks, and other European powers. Their empire ultimately declined in the late-9th-century A.D., largely due to pressure from the Franks and other neighboring groups.
[Pohl, Walter. *The Avars: A Steppe Empire in Central Europe*. (Oxford: Oxford University Press, A.D. 2018), pp. 72-73.]

Assault, Accusation, and Vindication

In A.D. 799, Pope Leo III became the target of a violent

conspiracy, likely fueled by jealousy, ambition, and lingering

resentment among the relatives of his predecessor, *Pope Adrian I.*[62]

During the solemn procession of the Greater Litanies on 25 April, as

Leo approached *the Flaminian Gate,*[63] a group of armed conspirators

launched a brutal assault. Dragged to the ground, Leo was viciously

attacked—his assailants attempting to tear out his eyes and remove

his tongue, leaving him bloodied and half-dead in the street.

Under the cover of night, he was taken to the monastery of

St. Erasmus on the Celian Hill, one of the seven hills of Rome.

Miraculously, Leo recovered the full use of both his sight and

speech—an event later regarded as divine intervention. Escaping

---

[62] **Pope Adrian I:** (reigned A.D. 772–795), was the pope who preceded Leo III. He played a key role in the strengthening of the papacy, particularly through his relationship with Charlemagne, which would later become crucial for Leo III's own rise to power. Adrian I's papacy saw the consolidation of the Papal States and a firm stance against the Lombards, as well as an important role in the development of the Christian church's liturgy and artwork.
  [Schuster, Ildefonso. *The History of the Church of Rome.* (London: Burns & Oates, A.D. 1920), pp. 283-284.]

[63] **The Flaminian Gate:** (*Porta Flaminia*), was one of the gates of ancient Rome, located along the Via Flaminia. It was situated on the northern edge of the city and was a key route for travelers and military. The gate also had symbolic importance, often linked to major processions and religious events, such as the Greater Litanies, which were celebrated with solemnity and ceremony.
  [Talbert, Richard J. A. *Atlas of the Roman World.* (New York: Oxford University Press, A.D. 1981), p. 112.]

captivity, he fled north to seek the aid of Charlemagne, accompanied by a loyal band of Romans. Despite the slanderous accusations already whispered into the Frankish king's ears, Leo was received with great honor at *Paderborn.*[64]

After several months, Charlemagne arranged for Leo to be safely escorted back to Rome, where the pope was welcomed with widespread celebration by both locals and foreigners. Charlemagne dispatched envoys to investigate the matter, and the pope's accusers—unable to prove Leo's guilt or clear their own names—were sent as prisoners to *Frankland.*[65] The following year, in A.D. 800, Charlemagne arrived in Rome and convened a formal inquiry. The assembled bishops, citing ecclesiastical precedent, declared that

---

[64] **Paderborn:** is a city in modern-day Germany, which became an important center for the Carolingian Empire. It was the site of several meetings between Charlemagne and his allies, including Pope Leo III. The city held significance as a base for Charlemagne's political and military activities, and it is where Pope Leo sought refuge after his violent attack in Rome.
[Fried, Johannes. *Charlemagne.* (Cambridge: Polity Press, A.D. 2009), pp. 122-124.]

[65] **Frankland:** refers to the territory or realm of the Franks, which during the reign of Charlemagne included a large part of Western Europe, notably modern France, Germany, the Low Countries, and parts of Italy. The term "Frankland" was often used to describe the regions controlled by the Frankish kingdom, especially under the Carolingian dynasty. Charlemagne, King of the Franks, expanded this domain significantly, establishing a powerful empire that played a central role in the medieval history of Europe.
[Sawyer, Peter H. *The Oxford Illustrated History of the Vikings.* (Oxford: Oxford University Press, A.D. 1997), pp. 134-135.]

no earthly authority could judge a pope. Nevertheless, Leo voluntarily swore an oath of innocence to clear his name and ease public doubts. At his request, the death sentences passed on his main conspirators were reduced to exile, a gesture of mercy that reflected the strength and clemency of his character.

The Crown, the Creed, and the Cross

Just days after his public vindication, Pope Leo III and Charlemagne met again—this time in a moment that would alter the course of history. On Christmas Day, in the grandeur of St. Peter's Basilica, after the Gospel had been sung, Leo approached the Frankish king, who knelt in reverence before the Confession of St. Peter. With solemn ceremony, the pope placed a crown upon his head. At once, the basilica thundered with acclaim: *"To Charles, the most pious Augustus, crowned by God, to our great and pacific emperor, life and victory!"*[66]

With this dramatic act, the Roman Empire in the West was reborn. In principle, the Church had now proclaimed a unified temporal authority on earth, parallel to the singular spiritual head

---

[66] Einhard. *The Life of Charlemagne, trans. Samuel E. W. F. Lane.* (New York: Frederick Ungar Publishing Co., A.D. 1960), p. 103.

established by Christ. As emperor, Charlemagne's first duty was understood to be the protector of the Church and Christendom against external threats. Pope Leo, ever eager to reconcile East and West under one empire, supported a proposed marriage between Charlemagne and the Eastern *Empress Irene.*[67] But her deposition in A.D. 801 extinguished any hope of that union.

Three years after Charlemagne's departure from Rome, Leo journeyed across the Alps to visit him once more, likely to discuss the planned division of Charlemagne's empire among his sons. By A.D. 806, Leo had been invited to give his formal assent to the emperor's partitioning provisions. Their collaboration extended into ecclesiastical matters as well. While both opposed the Spanish heresy of *Adoptionism,*[68] Charlemagne, more assertive in theology, sought the

---

[67] **Empress Irene of Athens:** (A.D. 752–803), was a Byzantine empress who ruled as regent for her son, Emperor Constantine VI, before deposing him and ruling as the sole empress. Her reign is most notable for her efforts to restore the veneration of icons after the Iconoclast Controversy. She is also remembered for being the first woman to hold the title of Empress of the Romans in her own right. Her rule ended when she was exiled by a coup in A.D. 802.

   [Angold, Michael. *The Byzantine Empire: A Political History.* (London: Routledge, A.D. 2006), pp. 133-134.]

[68] **Adoptionism:** was a theological doctrine that arose in the early Middle Ages, particularly in Spain. It taught that Jesus Christ was adopted as the Son of God at his baptism or resurrection, rather than being the eternal Son of God. This view was condemned as heretical by the Church, as it contradicted the traditional Christian understanding of the Trinity and the nature of Christ's divinity. Adoptionism was notably promoted by figures like the Spanish theologian Elipandus of Toledo.

universal inclusion of the *Filioque*[69] in the Nicene Creed—going further than Leo, who held more cautiously to tradition.

Nonetheless, their joint efforts bore wide-reaching fruit. They raised Salzburg to metropolitical status in Bavaria, and compensated Fortunatus of Grado with the bishopric of Pola after he lost his original see. Their influence stretched even to England: with their intervention, King Eardulf was restored to the throne of Northumbria, and a long-standing dispute between Archbishop Eanbald of York and Archbishop Wulfred of Canterbury was finally resolved.

Papal Authority in the Britannica

Pope Leo III maintained strong and independent relations with the English Church, apart from his alliance with Charlemagne. At his direction, the Synod of Clovesho was held in A.D. 803 in the

---

[Batton, Bernard F. *The Early Christian Doctrine of the Trinity.* (London: Epworth Press, A.D. 1953), pp. 155-157.]

[69] **Filioque:** was a theological dispute between the Eastern and Western Christian churches regarding the phrase "and the Son" in the Nicene Creed. The Western Church, particularly the Latin-speaking Church, added *Filioque* to the creed, stating that the Holy Spirit proceeds "from the Father and the Son." The Eastern Church rejected this addition, arguing that the Holy Spirit proceeds solely from the Father. This disagreement contributed to the schism between the Eastern Orthodox and Roman Catholic Churches in A.D. 1054.

[Meyendorff, John. *Byzantine Theology: Historical Trends and Doctrinal Themes.* (New York: Fordham University Press, A.D. 1983), pp. 104-107.]

Kingdom of Mercia of Anglo-Saxon England and issued a
condemnation of the growing practice of appointing laymen as heads
of monasteries—an abuse Leo sought to curb in defense of monastic
integrity.

Responding to the appeals of *Ethelheard*,[70] Archbishop of
Canterbury, Leo took further decisive action. He excommunicated
Eadbert Praen for unlawfully seizing the throne of Kent and revoked
the pallium previously granted to the See of Lichfield. This action
restored ecclesiastical jurisdiction to Canterbury, affirming the
original structure arranged by *St. Gregory the Great*,[71] "the Apostle and
Master of the nation of the English."

---

[70] **Ethelheard:** the Archbishop of Canterbury from A.D. 773 until his death in
A.D. 805. He was instrumental in securing the stability of the Christian church in
England during the reign of King Offa of Mercia. Ethelheard played a key role in
the ecclesiastical politics of his time, including his support of the Papal authority
and the establishment of relations with the Carolingian Empire. He is also noted
for his participation in the Synod of Clovesho in A.D. 803.
　　[Finberg, H. P. R. *The History of Anglo-Saxon England.* (London: Routledge,
　　A.D. 1974), pp. 167-168.]

[71] **St. Gregory the Great:** (A.D. 540–604), was one of the most influential popes in
early medieval Christianity. His papacy (A.D. 590–604) was marked by efforts to
reform the church, promote monasticism, and spread Christianity, particularly in
England. Gregory is also famous for sending missionaries, such as Augustine of
Canterbury, to evangelize the Anglo-Saxons. His writings, including *Dialogues* and
Moralia on Job, remain significant in Christian theology.
　　[Chadwick, Henry. *The Early Church.* (London: Penguin Books, A.D.
　　1993), pp. 203-205.]

The Legacy of Pope Leo

Leo's involvement did not end there. He was also drawn into the bitter disputes between *Archbishop Wulfred*[72] and *King Cenulf*[73] of Mercia. Though the precise causes of their conflict remain obscure, Wulfred appears to have borne the greater burden. With papal approval, Cenulf managed to have the archbishop suspended from exercising his episcopal office and placed the kingdom under a kind of ecclesiastical interdict for six years. Driven by avarice, Cenulf continued to persecute Wulfred and even targeted the monastery of Abingdon. Only after extracting a large payment from its abbot did he relent—proclaiming, as he claimed, at the request of "the lord

---

[72] **Archbishop Wulfred:** was the Archbishop of Canterbury from A.D. 803 to 832. He played a prominent role in the ecclesiastical and political life of Anglo-Saxon England, including his involvement in the reforms of the church in the early-9th-century A.D. His tenure was marked by attempts to strengthen the authority of the Archbishopric of Canterbury, especially in light of the power of the Mercian kings. He was also involved in the disputes over the primacy of Canterbury over the other English sees, notably during the reign of King Cenwulf.

[Dumville, David. *Wulfred, Archbishop of Canterbury: His Life and Times.* (Cambridge: Cambridge University Press, A.D. 1985), pp. 72-75.]

[73] **King Cenulf:** was the King of Mercia from A.D. 796 to 821. His reign followed the powerful rule of King Offa and saw both a decline in Mercian dominance and the strengthening of the kingdom's Christian institutions. Cenulf worked to maintain Mercian independence and also had significant interactions with the Anglo-Saxon church, including support for Archbishop Wulfred of Canterbury. His reign was marked by both internal struggles and external pressures from neighboring kingdoms.

[Jones, Michael H. *The Kings of Mercia.* (Oxford: Oxford University Press, A.D. 2000), pp. 56-58.]

Apostolic and most glorious Pope Leo," the monastery's inviolable

status.

Byzantine Monks

During Pope Leo III's pontificate, the Church of

Constantinople was roiled by tension and controversy. Monastic life

flourished under the leadership of figures like *St. Theodore the Studite,*[74]

yet these monks grew increasingly wary of what they perceived as the

lenient and compromising stance of their patriarch, *Tarasius.*[75] Their

discontent deepened in response to the scandalous behavior of

Emperor Constantine VI,[76] who divorced his wife Maria to marry a

---

[74] **St. Theodore the Studite:** (A.D. 759–826), was a Byzantine monk, theologian, and abbot of the Studion Monastery in Constantinople. He became a leading figure in the defense of icon veneration during the second phase of the Iconoclastic Controversy, especially under the reign of Emperor Leo V. His writings emphasized the independence of the Church from imperial interference and strongly opposed any form of compromise with heresy, especially in relation to the Filioque and imperial-appointed patriarchs.
   [Talbot, Alice-Mary. *St. Theodore the Studite: His Life and Times.* (Washington, D.C.: Dumbarton Oaks, A.D. 1991), pp. 45–52.]
[75] **Tarasius:** (A.D. 730–806), was Patriarch of Constantinople from A.D. 784 to 806. A layman and imperial secretary before his elevation, Tarasius played a key role in the Second Council of Nicaea (A.D. 787), which restored the veneration of icons after the first period of Byzantine Iconoclasm. Though later criticized by some—especially Theodore the Studite—for his leniency toward imperial interference in ecclesiastical matters, his leadership marked a significant step in the reconciliation of Church and empire.
   [Herrin, Judith. *Byzantium: The Surprising Life of a Medieval Empire.* (Princeton University Press, A.D. 2007), pp. 132–135.]
[76] **Emperor Constantine IV:** (reigned A.D. 780–797), was the only son of Emperor Leo IV and Empress Irene. He initially reigned under the regency of his mother and later attempted to assert his authority, leading to tensions over both

woman named Theodota. Though Patriarch Tarasius voiced disapproval of the emperor's actions, he refused to excommunicate Constantine—hoping to avoid greater turmoil—much to the indignation of the monastic community.

In retaliation for their outspoken opposition to his illicit marriage, Constantine subjected many of the monks to imprisonment and exile. When further unrest erupted over the reinstatement of a priest who had officiated at the emperor's unlawful union— previously degraded by Tarasius—the monks again suffered for their resistance. In their persecution, they turned to Pope Leo for support.

Leo responded with more than mere words. He sent the monks letters filled with praise and encouragement, accompanied by generous material gifts to aid them in their suffering. His solidarity with the Byzantine monks reinforced his role as a universal shepherd of the Church. Later, when *Michael I*[77] succeeded Constantine VI, Leo

---

religious and political matters. His controversial second marriage and conflicts with the monastic community—particularly St. Theodore the Studite—damaged his support. He was ultimately deposed and blinded by Irene, who then ruled as empress in her own right.

> [Treadgold, Warren. *A History of the Byzantine State and Society.* (Stanford: Stanford University Press, A.D. 1997), pp. 379–392.]

[77] **Michael I:** (reigned A.D. 811–813), the son-in-law of Byzantine Emperor Nicephorus I, came to power after the latter's death in battle. Known for his piety and deference to the Church, he supported icon veneration and maintained favorable relations with ecclesiastical authorities like Patriarch Nikephoros and St.

confirmed a treaty between the new emperor and Charlemagne,

establishing a tenuous peace between East and West and affirming

the pope's influence across both spheres of Christendom.

After Charlemagne

In all major affairs of his pontificate, Pope Leo III worked

closely with Charlemagne, the Frankish emperor. It was on

Charlemagne's counsel that Leo took decisive action to protect the

Papal States from *Saracen*[78] incursions. To safeguard the coasts, he

maintained a fleet and ordered regular naval patrols. Yet recognizing

---

Theodore the Studite. His reign ended after a military defeat by the Bulgars, leading
to his abdication in favor of Leo V the Armenian.

[Haldon, John. *Byzantium in the Iconoclast Era (c. 680–850): A History.*
(Cambridge: Cambridge University Press, A.D. 2010), pp. 347–350.]

[78] **Saracen:** was a term used by Christian writers to describe Muslim forces,
particularly those from North Africa and the eastern Mediterranean. Originally, it
likely derived from the Greek *Sarakenoi*, a name for certain Arab tribes in the Sinai
and surrounding deserts during Late Antiquity. By the 8th- and 9th-centuries A.D.,
it commonly referred to Muslim raiders who launched attacks on southern Europe,
including Italy and the islands of the western Mediterranean. Medieval Christians,
however, interpreted the term *Saracen* theologically, believing it meant "not from
Sarah" — a reference to the biblical idea that Muslims descended from Ishmael,
the son of Abraham and Hagar, rather than from Isaac, Sarah's son. Muhammad's
lineage was thus understood as stemming from Ishmael, distinguishing Muslims as
not part of the "true" Abrahamic covenant in Christian thought.

[McCormick, Michael. *Origins of the European Economy: Communications and
Commerce, A.D. 300–900.* (Cambridge: Cambridge University Press, A.D.
2001), pp. 410–412.]

his limited capacity to defend the distant island of *Corsica*[79] from Muslim pirates, he entrusted its protection to the emperor.

With Charlemagne's military and political support, Leo also succeeded in reclaiming papal lands near Gaeta and restored their governance under his appointed rectors. The close alliance with the emperor allowed the pope to strengthen the Church's position both spiritually and territorially. However, Charlemagne's death on January 28, A.D. 814, marked a turning point.

Without the emperor's protection, Leo faced renewed internal threats. A fresh conspiracy arose against him, but this time the plot was uncovered before it could unfold. Leo responded swiftly, having the ringleaders arrested and executed. Yet danger persisted. Not long after, rebellious nobles from the *Campagna region*[80] rose up and began plundering the countryside. They advanced toward Rome, but were

---

[79] **Corsica:** a strategically important island in the western Mediterranean, was subject to repeated Saracen raids in the early-9th-century A.D. Lacking the naval power to secure it, Pope Leo III sought help from Charlemagne, who accepted its defense as part of the Carolingian Empire's responsibilities.
  [Noble, Thomas F. X. *The Republic of St. Peter: The Birth of the Papal State, 680–825.* (Philadelphia: University of Pennsylvania Press, A.D. 1984), pp. 231–233.]

[80] **Campagna region:** refers to the low-lying plains surrounding Rome, which in the early Middle Ages was sparsely populated and often lawless. It was notorious for noble feuds and frequent revolts, posing constant challenges to papal authority.
  [Wickham, Chris. *Early Medieval Italy: Central Power and Local Society, 400–1000.* (London: Macmillan, A.D. 1981), pp. 104–106.]

decisively defeated by the Duke of *Spoleto*,[81] who acted under the authority of the King of Italy (*Langobardia*).[82]

Charlemagne's generous financial support had fortified not just Leo's defenses, but also his charitable and artistic endeavors. Leo used these resources to care for the poor, restore churches throughout Rome and as far as Ravenna, and commission beautiful works of sacred art. Notably, he employed mosaic—an enduring medium—to both commemorate his alliance with Charlemagne and enrich the beauty of the Church. His titular church, St. Susanna, was especially adorned, and a mosaic portrait of Pope Leo remained there until the end of the 16th-century A.D., a lasting testament to his legacy.

---

[81] **Spoleto:** located in central Italy, was a powerful Lombard territory that often acted semi-independently. In the early-9th-century A.D., the dukes of Spoleto served as key military allies of the papacy and the Carolingian rulers, helping suppress uprisings in the region.

[Delogu, Paolo. *An Introduction to the History of Medieval Italy (trans. Matthew Moran.* (Cambridge: Cambridge University Press, A.D. 2002), pp. 144–145.]

[82] **Langobardia:** or Lombardy, referred originally to the territory ruled by the Lombards in Italy. After Charlemagne's conquest in A.D. 774, it became a Frankish kingdom known as the Kingdom of Italy, with Frankish kings retaining the Lombard legacy and titles.

[McKitterick, Rosamond. *The Frankish Kingdoms under the Carolingians, 751–987.* (London: Longman, A.D. 1983), pp. 84–85.]

Legacy and Veneration

Pope Leo III died on June 12, A.D. 816, and was buried in St. Peter's Basilica. His relics rest alongside those of other pontiffs bearing his name—Sts. Leo I, Leo II, and Leo IV—marking his enduring place in the legacy of the Church. Centuries later, in A.D. 1673, he was officially canonized, confirming his veneration as a saint.

Among the tangible remnants of his papacy are the silver denarii still in existence today. These coins bear not only the name of Pope Leo but also that of the Frankish emperor, a testament to their close alliance. The shared inscription symbolizes the emperor's role as protector of the Church and overlord of the city of Rome, reflecting the political and spiritual bond that shaped a new era in Western Christendom.

Chapter IV

Pope Leo IV (A.D. 847-855)

The Defense of Rome

A native Roman and the son of Radoald, Leo IV was unanimously elected to succeed Pope Sergius II. In response to the recent and alarming Saracen attack on Rome in A.D. 846, the people, fearing further devastation, moved quickly. Leo was consecrated on April 10, A.D. 847, even before receiving the emperor's approval.

He received his early education in Rome at the monastery of St. Martin, near St. Peter's. His devout conduct attracted the attention of Pope Gregory IV, who appointed him a subdeacon. Later, under Sergius II, he was elevated to Cardinal-Priest of the Church of the Quatuor Coronati.

Though reluctant to assume the papacy, Leo immediately set

about strengthening the city's defenses. Determined to prevent another Saracen raid, he began restoring and reinforcing the city walls, rebuilding fifteen major towers. Most notably, *he became the first to enclose the Vatican Hill with a defensive wall.* Funding came from the emperor, while manpower and additional support came from the cities and agricultural colonies throughout the Duchy of Rome.

After four years of labor, the fortifications were completed in A.D. 852. The newly protected district became known as the *Leonine City,* named in his honor. Pope Leo IV solemnly blessed the new defenses, marking a critical achievement in the safeguarding of the Eternal City.

Restorer of the Eternal City

While the work of refortifying Rome was still underway, a formidable Saracen fleet—likely sailing from Sardinia—set its course for the city. In A.D. 849, however, it was decisively destroyed off the coast of Ostia by the combined naval forces of Rome, Naples, Amalfi, and Gaeta, aided by a providential storm.

Following the completion of the city walls, Pope Leo IV undertook the rebuilding of Portus, the ancient harbor of Rome, and settled there a group of Corsican exiles who had been driven from their homeland by Saracen devastation. Inspired by his example and exhortations, other towns within the Duchy of Rome were also fortified.

Leo worked tirelessly to repair the damage inflicted by the Saracen raid of A.D. 846, particularly to the city's churches. St. Peter's Basilica had suffered greatly; although its former grandeur was never fully restored, Leo managed to enhance parts of it, rendering them even more beautiful than before. He also oversaw the renovation of many significant sites: St. Martin's, where he had studied; the Quatuor Coronati, where he had once served as priest; the Lateran Palace; the Anglo-Saxon Borgo; Subiaco; and numerous other locations in and around Rome.

Among his notable architectural contributions was the construction of the Church of Santa Maria Nova. It was built to replace Santa Maria Antiqua, which had fallen into disrepair and was threatened by the collapsing ruins of the Palace of the Caesars—a site whose remains have only recently been rediscovered.

Leo's influence extended beyond Rome. In A.D. 850, he

crowned *Louis,*[83] the son of Emperor Lothair, thereby associating him

with imperial power. Three years later, he received the young *Alfred of*

Wessex,[84] whom he anointed and adopted as his spiritual son. "He

hallowed the child Alfred to king," records an old English historian,

"by anointing; and receiving him for his own child by adoption, gave

him confirmation, and sent him back [to England] with the blessing

of St. Peter the Apostle."

Final Acts of Authority

In A.D. 853, Pope Leo IV convened a significant synod in

Rome. The council enacted various decrees aimed at strengthening

ecclesiastical discipline and promoting learning. Among its notable

actions was the condemnation of *Anastasius,*[85] the defiant Cardinal of

---

[83] **Louis II:** (A.D. 825–875), was the eldest son of Lothair I, Emperor of the
Romans, and became co-emperor with his father in A.D. 850. Pope Leo IV
crowned him in Rome to strengthen ties between the papacy and the Carolingian
dynasty. This act reinforced the papal role in imperial legitimacy.
   [Nelson, Janet L. *The Frankish World, 750–900.* (London: Hambledon
   Press, A.D. 1996), pp. 258–260.]
[84] **Alfred of Wessex:** (later King Alfred the Great), traveled to Rome in A.D. 853
as a young boy. According to Asser's *Life of King Alfred*, Pope Leo IV "hallowed the
child Alfred to king" by anointing and adopting him as his spiritual son. This
gesture symbolized a sacred blessing and perhaps foreshadowed Alfred's future
kingship.
   [Asser, *Life of King Alfred, trans. Simon Keynes and Michael Lapidge in Alfred the
   Great: Asser's Life of King Alfred and Other Contemporary Sources.* (London:
   Penguin Classics, A.D. 1983), pp. 71–72.]
[85] **Anastasius:** was Cardinal of St. Marcellus and former Librarian of the Roman
Church, was condemned for his insubordination and refusal to recognize papal

Pope Leo IV

St. Marcellus and former librarian of the Roman Church.

At the same time, rebellious behavior from *John*,[86] the Archbishop of Ravenna, compelled Leo to journey personally to the city. His goal was to restore obedience to ecclesiastical law and discipline among John and his allies. A similar mission of correction led him into correspondence with Hincmar, the influential Archbishop of Reims. It was while engaged in these efforts to uphold the dignity and unity of the Church that Leo died.

Another challenge during Leo's papacy came from Nomenoe, the ambitious Duke of Brittany. Seeking independence from imperial control, Nomenoe openly defied both Pope Leo and *King Charles the Bald*.[87] He deposed several bishops, appointed new ones, and subordinated them to a metropolitan see of his own invention at Dol.

---

authority. Though later reinstated under Pope Nicholas I, during Leo IV's pontificate he was declared deposed by a Roman synod.

[Richards, Jeffrey. *The Popes and the Papacy in the Early Middle Ages: 476–752.* (London: Routledge & Kegan Paul, A.D. 1979), pp. 248–250.]

[86] **John, Archbishop of Ravenna**: was known for resisting papal authority and asserting greater independence over his see. Pope Leo IV personally intervened in Ravenna to address John's defiance and restore canonical discipline.

[Mann, Horace K. *The Lives of the Popes in the Early Middle Ages, Vol. 4.* (London: Kegan Paul, Trench, Trübner & Co., A.D. 1910), pp. 156–158.]

[87] **Hincmar of Reims**: (A.D. 806–882), a major ecclesiastical and political figure in the Carolingian Empire, frequently corresponded with the papacy. Leo IV communicated with Hincmar on matters of Church discipline and orthodoxy, including clerical conduct and episcopal authority.

[Nelson, Janet L. *Charles the Bald.* (London: Longman, A.D. 1992), pp. 209–211.]

This irregular arrangement would persist until the 13th-century A.D., when the Archbishop of Tours finally regained jurisdiction over the Breton sees.

Leo also found himself navigating a complex dispute in the East. *St. Methodius,*[88] the Patriarch of Constantinople, had suspended *Gregory Asbestas,*[89] Bishop of Syracuse, for consecrating a bishop outside his own diocese. When St. Ignatius succeeded Methodius, he barred Gregory from attending his own consecration. In retaliation, Gregory rebelled. Ignatius deposed him and appealed to Pope Leo to confirm the decision. Leo, however, declined. He argued that Ignatius had acted without informing Rome, having neither

---

[88] **St. Methodius I:** (A.D. 787–847), served as Patriarch of Constantinople from A.D. 843 to 847. He played a pivotal role in ending the second period of Byzantine Iconoclasm and restoring the veneration of icons. A devout monk and theologian, he was appointed patriarch by Empress Theodora and is commemorated as a saint in both the Eastern Orthodox and Roman Catholic traditions. His ecclesiastical leadership also included administrative actions such as the suspension of bishops, including Gregory Asbestas, as part of broader efforts to reform clerical conduct.
   [Gregory, Timothy E. *A History of Byzantium, 2nd ed.* (Chichester: Wiley-Blackwell, A.D. 2010), p. 227.]

[89] **Gregory Asbestas:** was a prominent 9th-century A.D. bishop who served multiple terms as Archbishop of Syracuse and later as Metropolitan of Nicaea. A protégé of Methodius I, Gregory became a leading opponent of Methodius' successor, Ignatius. After being suspended by Methodius for unauthorized episcopal consecrations, Gregory's tensions with Ignatius escalated when Ignatius barred him from attending his own consecration. In retaliation, Gregory denounced Ignatius, leading to his excommunication in A.D. 854. Gregory appealed to Pope Leo IV, citing the right of appeal to Rome as established by the Council of Sardica.
   [Dvornik, Francis. *The Photian Schism: History and Legend.* (Cambridge: Cambridge University Press, A.D. 1948), pp. 44–46.]

summoned papal legates nor received papal letters—actions that disregarded proper protocol and papal primacy.

summoned papal legates nor received papal letters—actions that disregarded proper protocol and papal primacy.

Despite his opposition to Patriarch Ignatius, Leo faced suspicion at home. One of his own high-ranking military officials, Daniel—a *magister militum*—accused him before Emperor Louis II of plotting to replace Frankish influence with Greek alliances. Leo swiftly disproved the charge, persuading Louis of his loyalty. Daniel was sentenced to death, but escaped execution through the emperor's clemency.

Shortly thereafter, Pope Leo IV passed away and was buried in St. Peter's Basilica on 17 July, A.D. 855. His reputation for holiness endured beyond his death. Both his biographer and the *Patriarch Photius*[90] attested to his miracles, and his name was entered into the Roman Martyrology.

---

[90] **Patriarch Photius I of Constantinople:** was a central figure in the 9th-century A.D., known for his intellectual contributions, his leadership during the Photian Schism, and his role in defending the independence of the Eastern Church against papal encroachment. His testimony regarding the miracles of Pope Leo IV highlights the ongoing influence of Leo's sanctity in both religious and political circles, even after his death. Photius's writings and actions had a lasting impact on the theological and ecclesiastical landscape of Byzantium and the wider Christian world.

[Meyendorff, John. *The Byzantine Empire: A Historical and Cultural Overview.* (New York: Cambridge University Press, A.D. 1987), p. 212.]

Chapter V

Pope Leo V (A.D. 903)

Life of Pope Leo V

Very little is known about Pope Leo V, and much of his papacy remains a mystery. The exact date of his election to the papacy is uncertain, but it is highly probable that he was pope in August A.D. 903. His reign is one of the shortest in papal history, lasting only about a month, and his life before his election is scarcely documented.

Leo was a native of Priapi, a small town in the district of Ardea, located not far from Rome. Unlike many of his papal predecessors, he was not a Cardinal-Priest of the city but was attached to a church outside Rome, earning him the title *presbiter forensis*[91] in contemporary papal catalogues. His rise to the papacy was unexpected, given his relatively humble ecclesiastical position at the time of his election.

Although his papacy was brief, Leo V was described by *Auxilius,*[92] a contemporary writer, as "a man of God and of praiseworthy life and holiness." According to Auxilius, he held the "rudder of the Holy Roman Church" for just thirty days, yet his character and piety left an impression on those who knew him. Despite his reputation for holiness, little else is known about his actions during his short reign. The only papal decree attributed to

---

[91] **presbiter forensis:** (literally, "rural priest" or "external presbyter"), refers to a clergyman not assigned to one of the titular churches of Rome proper but rather to a church in the surrounding rural or suburban areas. In the context of papal elections, this designation indicated a lower-ranking or less politically connected ecclesiastical status, making Leo V's elevation to the papacy notably unusual. Papal catalogues of the early-10th-century A.D. identify Leo V as a presbiter forensis, suggesting he was not part of the influential Roman ecclesiastical elite at the time of his election.
[Levillain, Philippe. *The Papacy: An Encyclopedia, trans. Virginia L. Collins, Vol. 2.* (New York: Routledge, A.D. 2002), p. 993.]

[92] **Auxilius of Naples:** was a cleric and defender of papal legitimacy during the late-9th- and early-10th-centuries A.D., known especially for his opposition to the interference of secular rulers in ecclesiastical appointments. A contemporary of Pope Leo V, Auxilius praised Leo as "a man of God and of praiseworthy life and holiness," and recorded that he governed the Church for "just thirty days." Though brief, Auxilius's testimony is one of the few near-contemporary sources affirming Leo's virtue and the brevity of his pontificate.
[Auxilius of Naples, *Tractatus de Ordinatione a Laicis Facienda,* in *Monumenta Germaniae Historica, Libelli de Lite Imperatorum et Pontificum, ed. Emil Dümmler Vol. 1.* (Hannover: Hahn, A.D. 1891), pp. 85–87.]

him is a Bull that exempted the canons of Bologna from paying taxes, though no other significant acts or decisions have been recorded.

The circumstances of Leo V's death are as enigmatic as his papacy. After serving as pope for just over a month, he was seized by *Christopher*,[93] the Cardinal-Priest of St. Damasus, and imprisoned. Christopher, who would go on to declare himself antipope, quickly took the papal throne for himself. However, his claim to the papacy was short-lived, as he was soon displaced by Sergius III, who would reign as pope from A.D. 904 to 911.

Various accounts suggest that Sergius III, upon taking the papal chair, may have shown some "pity" for Leo and Christopher, both of whom were imprisoned. One source even claims that Sergius caused both men to be put to death. However, it seems more likely that Leo V died a natural death either in prison or while in exile, possibly in a monastery, rather than being executed.

---

[93] **Christopher of Damasus:** is considered an antipope by most modern historians, though he was at one time included in some medieval papal lists. He deposed Leo V under obscure and likely violent circumstances, imprisoning him and seizing the papacy around late A.D. 903. Christopher's legitimacy remains contested, particularly given the chaotic political conditions in Rome at the time and his swift displacement by Pope Sergius III, who later assumed the papal throne with the backing of Theophylact of Tusculum.

[Mann, Horace K. *The Lives of the Popes in the Early Middle Ages, Vol. 4: The Popes in the Days of Feudal Anarchy, 891–999.* (London: Kegan Paul, Trench, Trübner & Co., A.D. 1910), pp. 197–201.]

Pope Leo V

The lack of definitive records surrounding Leo V's life, pontificate, and death has led to much speculation among historians. His papacy, though brief and largely unremarkable in terms of actions, stands as a poignant example of the political turmoil and intrigue that characterized the papacy during the early-10th-century A.D. Despite the uncertainty surrounding his tenure, Leo V's name remains etched in the annals of history, a fleeting figure in the turbulent history of the papacy.

Chapter VI

Pope Leo VI (A.D. 928)

A Brief Pontificate

The exact dates of Pope Leo VI's election and death remain uncertain, but it is generally accepted that he served as pope during the latter half of A.D. 928. Some scholars believe he was elected in June of that year and reigned for a brief period of seven months and five days, passing away in February A.D. 929. However, there are alternative theories suggesting that he may have been elected before June, adding to the ambiguity surrounding his papacy.

Leo VI was a Roman by birth, named Leo from the beginning, the son of Christopher, who had served as the *primicerius* (chief of staff) under *Pope John VIII*.[94] Christopher had also been a

---

[94] **Pope John VIII:** (reigned A.D. 872–882), is remembered as one of the most vigorous and embattled pontiffs of the early Middle Ages. His papacy was marked

prominent political figure, functioning as the prime minister of John VIII. With such a background, Leo VI was deeply embedded in the political workings of the Church. Before becoming pope, Leo held the position of Cardinal-Priest of St. Susanna, a significant ecclesiastical office in Rome.

Upon his election as pope, Leo VI inherited a papacy still reeling from the turbulent reign of his predecessor, *John X.*[95] John X had been engaged in several pressing matters, notably ecclesiastical jurisdiction disputes in Dalmatia. These disputes continued to require resolution after Leo VI ascended to the papacy. In response to these challenges, Pope Leo VI issued a decree granting the pallium to Archbishop John of Spalato. He also instructed all Dalmatian bishops

---

by military and diplomatic efforts to resist Saracen incursions in southern Italy and by attempts to maintain papal authority over the Frankish Church. Notably, he was the first pope known to have been assassinated, likely poisoned and then bludgeoned to death—a grim reflection of the political instability that plagued Rome during this era.

[Mann, Horace K. *The Lives of the Popes in the Early Middle Ages, Vol. 4.* (London: Kegan Paul, Trench, Trübner & Co., A.D. 1910), pp. 148–166.]

[95] **Pope John X:** (reigned A.D. 914–928), was an assertive and politically active pontiff whose reign was shaped by his alliances with secular rulers. He played a central role in organizing the Christian forces that defeated the Saracens at the Battle of the Garigliano in A.D. 915, a rare military success for the papacy. However, his papacy ended tragically when he was deposed and imprisoned by the powerful Roman noblewoman Marozia, ultimately dying under suspicious circumstances—likely murdered while in custody.

[Gregorovius, Ferdinand. *History of the City of Rome in the Middle Ages, Vol. 3,* trans. *Annie Hamilton.* (London: George Bell & Sons, A.D. 1896), pp. 216–223.]

to adhere to their diocesan boundaries and submit to the authority of Archbishop John. Additionally, he addressed the issue of Bishop Gregory, ordering him to limit his jurisdiction to the Diocese of Scodra.

Despite these important actions, there is very little else known about Leo VI's papacy. His time in office was short, and records of his reign are sparse. The most significant surviving document from his papacy is his papal Bull concerning ecclesiastical matters in Dalmatia, which sheds light on his administrative decisions and authority. Unfortunately, no other major reforms, actions, or controversies have been attributed to him.

The final years of Leo VI's life and papacy remain shrouded in mystery. According to most historical sources, he was buried in St. Peter's Basilica, though few details are known about the circumstances of his death or the events leading up to it. His brief tenure as pope was marked by efforts to settle ecclesiastical disputes, yet he remains a largely obscure figure in the history of the papacy.

In the broader context of papal history, Leo VI's reign is one of the many short-lived pontificates of the early-10th-century A.D., a period often characterized by political intrigue, brief papacies, and external pressures on the Church. Despite the lack of detailed records about his life and pontificate, Leo VI's papacy remains an integral part of this tumultuous era in the history of the Catholic Church.

Chapter VII

Pope Leo VII (A.D. 936-939)

Political Struggles and Reform

The date of Pope Leo VII's birth is unknown, but he died on 13 July, A.D. 939. A Roman by birth, he was named Leo from birth, following the pattern of his papal predecessors of the same name, none of whom had adopted "Leo" as a papal pseudonym. Before his election, he served as a priest at the Church of St. Sixtus on the Appian Way, one of the oldest titular churches in Rome, long associated with Christian worship and Benedictine monasticism.

Like Pope Leo IV, Leo VII was also a Benedictine monk, a fact reflected in the monastic tone of his pontificate. He was elected pope on January 3, A.D. 936, largely under the influence of *Alberic*

II,[96] who effectively controlled Rome's political affairs at the time.

Leo's ascent to the papacy was largely facilitated by the

powerful Roman prince and senator, Alberic, whose authority over

the city was challenged by *Hugo,*[97] the King of Italy (Langobardia).

The city of Rome itself was under siege by Hugo when the renowned

Abbot Odo of Cluny[98] arrived in the city. Odo, a figure known for his

significant influence over both Alberic and Hugo, had been

summoned by Pope Leo VII to help mediate peace between the

warring factions. Odo's diplomatic intervention proved successful,

---

[96] **Alberic II of Spoleto:** who ruled Rome from A.D. 932 to 954, not only controlled the city's political and military affairs but also effectively ruled the papal states through puppet popes. Remarkably, Alberic forbade the pope from leaving the city without his permission, underscoring his dominance over both secular and religious authority in Rome during his reign.
> [Norwich, John Julius. *The Popes: A History.* (Chatto & Windus, A.D. 2011), pp. 108-110.]

[97] **Hugo of Arles:** was King of Italy from A.D. 926 to 947, was originally a Burgundian noble who managed to claim the Italian crown through marriage. Interestingly, despite his ambitions in Italy, his power base remained largely in the Kingdom of Burgundy, and his Italian kingship was often challenged by local Roman nobility like Alberic II.
> [Reuter, Timothy. *The New Cambridge Medieval History: Vol. 3, c.900–c.1024.* (Cambridge University Press, A.D. 1999), pp. 584-586.]

[98] **Abbot Odo of Cluny:** was not only a key figure in monastic reform but also instrumental in spreading Cluniac influence across Europe, promoting the idea that monastic communities should be free from secular interference. Beyond his role in Rome, Odo founded several monasteries and was revered as a spiritual advisor by kings and popes alike, making him one of the most influential religious figures of the 10th-century A.D.
> [Leclerq, Jean. *Odo of Cluny: A Monastic Reformer.* (Cistercian Publications, A.D. 1982), pp. 105-113.]

leading to a temporary resolution of the conflict. A marriage between Alberic and Hugo's daughter, Alda, helped secure a fragile truce, thereby stabilizing the situation for the time being.

Pope Leo VII's papacy is marked primarily by his efforts to grant privileges and support to various monasteries, with a particular emphasis on Cluny. His papal Bulls reflect this focus, as he granted several privileges to Cluny and other monastic institutions. These actions aligned with the broader trend of monastic reform, which was gaining momentum across Europe at the time.

In addition to his support of monasticism, Pope Leo VII took significant steps to engage with reform efforts in Germany. During this period, *Emperor Henry I*[99] and his son, *Otto I,*[100] were

---

[99] **Emperor Henry I:** known as "the Fowler," was the first king of the Saxons and ruler of East Francia (Germany) from A.D. 919 to 936. Beyond his military successes in defending the kingdom against Magyar (Hungarian) invasions, Henry also prioritized the strengthening of Church institutions, recognizing the Church's role in consolidating royal authority and unifying the realm. His support for monastic reform and ecclesiastical discipline laid the groundwork for his son Otto's later more extensive Church reforms.

[Reuter, Timothy. *Germany in the Early Middle Ages c. 800–1056.* (Longman, A.D. 1991), pp. 78-82.]

[100] **Emperor Otto I:** king from A.D. 936 and emperor from A.D. 962, Otto significantly expanded imperial authority by closely aligning with the Church. He reinforced ecclesiastical discipline by appointing loyal bishops and abbots, using Church reform as a tool for political consolidation. His close cooperation with figures like Archbishop Frederick of Mainz demonstrated his commitment to upholding Church standards across Germany, culminating in the Ottonian Renaissance of religious and cultural revival.

working to strengthen the Church and enforce ecclesiastical discipline. Leo VII, recognizing the importance of these efforts, appointed Frederick, Archbishop of Mainz, as his vicar throughout all of Germany. This appointment granted Frederick the authority to take action against errant clerics, ensuring that the Church's moral and doctrinal standards were upheld across the German territories.

However, Pope Leo VII's reform efforts were not without controversy. One of his notable decisions was to refuse the request of Frederick to forcibly baptize Jews. While Leo did authorize the expulsion of Jews from cities if they refused to embrace Christianity, he did not condone the forced baptism of Jews, reflecting a more measured and cautious approach to religious conversion during his papacy.

Though Pope Leo VII's reign was relatively short, he was a significant figure in a time of political turbulence and ecclesiastical reform. His diplomatic skills, particularly in brokering peace between Alberic and Hugo, and his support for monastic reform, left a lasting impact on the Church. His papacy also contributed to the broader

---

[Leyser, Karl. *Communications and Power in Medieval Europe: The Carolingian and Ottonian Centuries.* (Hambledon Press, A.D. 1994), pp. 145-150.]

efforts to strengthen the Church's authority in Europe, particularly through his actions in Germany and his interactions with key figures like Archbishop Frederick.

In the larger context of papal history, Leo VII's pontificate is remembered for its efforts to navigate the complex political landscape of 10th-century A.D. Rome and for his role in advancing the cause of ecclesiastical reform. His death in A.D. 939 marked the end of a papacy defined by political intrigue, monastic support, and efforts to solidify Church authority in a turbulent time.

Chapter VIII

Pope Leo VIII (A.D. 963-965)

Imperial Intervention

The exact date of birth of Pope Leo VIII is unknown, and his death occurred between 20 February and 13 April A.D. 965. His pontificate, however, was deeply marked by political manipulation and imperial intervention, leaving a complex legacy in the annals of papal history.

Leo VIII was a Roman by birth, originally named Leo, the son of a man named John. His family was well known in the *Clivus Argentarii,* an area between the Corso and the Roman Forum—now the *Via di Marforio.* The family's prominence in this district suggests a degree of influence within the city's civic and ecclesiastical life. Before his unexpected elevation to the throne of St. Peter, Leo was associated with the protonotary, the senior administrative office in the Roman Curia, a role that brought him into the inner workings of the papacy and established his presence in Rome's clerical hierarchy.

His papacy was the direct result of the Emperor Otto I's controversial actions. In A.D. 963, Otto I deposed the notorious *Pope John XII,*[101] citing his immoral behavior and mismanagement of the papacy. This deposition was itself a breach of canonical law, as was Otto's subsequent imposition of a layman as his papal nominee. On 4 December, A.D. 963, Leo was chosen as pope, and by 6 December, he was consecrated as Bishop of Rome. Notably, the usual process for papal elections and ordinations was circumvented. Leo was hastily ordained by Sico, Bishop of Ostia, who performed the necessary ceremonies in violation of canonical norms.

Despite being elected under dubious circumstances, Leo's

---

[101] **Pope John XII:** (reigned A.D. 955–964), born Octavianus, was notorious for his scandalous behavior, including simony, political intrigue, and personal immorality. His papacy became so infamous that contemporaries accused him of turning the Lateran Palace into a brothel. His deposition by Emperor Otto I at the Synod of Rome in December, A.D. 963 marked a historic break from canon law, as no pope had previously been formally deposed by a secular ruler. John's removal was a turning point in imperial-papal relations and laid bare the tensions between Roman autonomy and imperial authority.

[Mann, Horace K. *The Lives of the Popes in the Early Middle Ages, Vol. 4: The Popes in the Days of Feudal Anarchy, 891–999.* (Kegan Paul, Trench, Trübner & Co., A.D. 1910), pp. 252–263.]

papacy began amidst a backdrop of growing tension between the Roman populace and the imperial authority of Otto I. A few weeks after his consecration, the Romans, discontent with imperial control, attempted to defy the emperor's authority. The rebellion was swiftly quashed by Otto, and as a result, the Romans faced severe punishment. However, Leo, in an attempt to preserve peace and secure the stability of Rome, interceded on behalf of the Romans, persuading Otto to return the hostages he had taken.

Leo's influence, however, was short-lived. Once Otto departed from Rome, the Romans rose again and expelled the pope he had installed. John XII, the previous pope who had been deposed, returned to the city and called for a synod to condemn Leo. He accused Leo of breaking faith and being a mere tool of imperial influence. In a dramatic move, John XII also deposed the clerics who had been ordained by Leo, effectively nullifying his papal authority in the eyes of the Roman populace.

Leo's fall from power, however, did not last long. On 14 May, A.D. 964, John XII died suddenly, creating a power vacuum. The

Romans, in a moment of poor judgment, elected *Benedict,*[102] a Cardinal-Deacon, as the new pope. Furious at the expulsion of Leo and the election of Benedict, Emperor Otto swiftly moved to assert his control over Rome once again. Otto's forces regained control of the city, and Benedict was soon arrested.

In a dramatic courtroom scene, Leo returned to Rome with the emperor and brought Benedict to trial. In a symbolic act of both authority and condemnation, Leo himself stripped Benedict of the papal pallium, reducing him to the rank of deacon. This public humiliation of Benedict signified Leo's restoration to power. The deposition was carried out with the tacit approval of the Roman clergy and, as some contemporaries report, Benedict himself may have acquiesced to his fate, acknowledging Leo's legitimacy as pope.

Thus, from July, A.D. 964 onwards, Leo VIII could be

---

[102] **Pope Benedict V:** was elected pope in May, A.D. 964 by the Roman populace shortly after the death of John XII, despite the fact that Emperor Otto I had already installed Leo VIII as his preferred pope. Known as *Benedictus Grammaticus* for his learning, Benedict had served as a Cardinal-Deacon before his controversial election. His papacy lasted barely a month before Otto's forces reentered Rome, deposed him, and reinstated Leo VIII. Although Otto spared Benedict's life, he was publicly degraded and exiled to Hamburg under the custody of Archbishop Adaldag, where he reportedly lived piously until his death.

[Mann, Horace K. *The Lives of the Popes in the Early Middle Ages, Vol. 4: The Popes in the Days of Feudal Anarchy, 891–999.* (Kegan Paul, Trench, Trübner & Co., A.D. 1910), pp. 278–285.]

considered the legitimate pope, though his reign remained largely
unremarkable. There are no surviving records of any significant
actions or reforms that Leo undertook during the remainder of his
papacy. It is claimed that Leo granted Emperor Otto the right to
appoint future popes and bishops, essentially cementing the imperial
control over papal elections. He also reportedly restored to Otto all
the lands that had been granted to the papacy by his predecessors.
However, it is widely believed that these documents were forged
during the later investiture controversy and may not reflect Leo's true
actions.

Leo VIII's papacy, although brief, was a reflection of the
turbulent relationship between the papacy and the Holy Roman
Empire during this period. His role as a pawn in the power struggles
of his time left little room for him to enact any meaningful change
within the Church. Nonetheless, the events of his papacy highlighted
the ongoing tension between secular rulers and the papacy, a dynamic
that would continue to shape the course of medieval Church history.

Leo VIII died in A.D. 965, with little more than a brief and
politically fraught reign to mark his papacy. His legacy is mostly
remembered for his involvement in the complex and often

contentious relationship between the imperial throne and the papacy,

as well as for his role in the series of papal intrigues and deposals that

defined this period in the history of Rome.

Chapter IX

Pope Leo IX (A.D. 1049-1054)

Early Life and Formation

Pope Leo IX, born Bruno on June 21, A.D. 1002, at

Egisheim near Colmar on the borders of Alsace, came from a noble

family that would later produce both saints and rulers. His father,

Hugh, was the first cousin of *Emperor Conrad*,[103] and both he and

Bruno's mother, Heilewide, were renowned for their piety and

learning.

From an early age, Bruno displayed a tender conscience. One

notable incident from his youth reflects this: although he

---

[103] **Emperor Conrad II:** (reigned A.D. 1024–1039), founder of the Salian dynasty, was the first German king to also be crowned Holy Roman Emperor in over a century. Known for his strong consolidation of imperial authority and legal reforms, he worked to stabilize the empire's frontiers and strengthen the position of the monarchy against rebellious dukes.
> [Weinfurter, Stefan. *The Salian Century: Main Currents in an Age of Transition.* *Translated by Barbara M. Bowlus.* (University of Pennsylvania Press, A.D. 1999), pp. 33–42.]

demonstrated a bright mind, he could not bring himself to study from a particularly beautiful book his mother had bought for him. It was later discovered that the book had been stolen from the Abbey of St. Hubert in the Ardennes. Once Heilewide had returned the stolen book to its rightful owners, Bruno's studies resumed without further hindrance.[104]

At the age of five, Bruno was entrusted to the care of Berthold, Bishop of Toul, who ran a school for noble youths. Bruno quickly became known for his intelligence, grace, and gracious nature, making him a favorite among his peers. However, a tragic event occurred during his youth when he was attacked by an animal while asleep at home, leaving him gravely injured and on the brink of death. During this time, Bruno experienced a vision of St. Benedict, who healed his wounds by touching them with a cross. This vision, which Bruno later recounted to his friends, was chronicled by Wibert, his close companion during his time as Bishop of Toul, and would be remembered as a significant moment in his early life.

---

[104] *Vita Brunonis, in Acta Sanctorum, Octobris I, ed. Jean Bolland et al.,* (Société des Bollandistes, 17th-century A.D).

Early Clerical Life and Rise to Bishop of Toul

Bruno's path to spiritual leadership began when he became *a canon*[105] of St. Stephen's at Toul in A.D. 1017. Despite his youth, he quickly earned a reputation for his calming influence, particularly with *Herimann,*[106] the choleric successor of Bishop Berthold. In A.D. 1024, when his cousin Conrad ascended to the throne as Emperor following the death of Henry I, Bruno's relatives sent him to serve in the king's court, where his virtuous character made a lasting impression. His companions, to distinguish him from others with the same name, began calling him "the good Bruno."

In A.D. 1026, Emperor Conrad, seeking to assert his authority in Italy, set out for the peninsula. With Bishop Herimann

---

[105] **A canon:** in the medieval Church was a cleric who lived according to the Rule of St. Augustine and served in a cathedral or collegiate church. Canons were responsible for liturgical services and the administration of the church's properties. Bruno's role as a canon at St. Stephen's Cathedral in Toul introduced him to both pastoral responsibilities and ecclesiastical governance, laying the foundation for his later reform efforts.

[Cowdrey, H. E. J. *The Cluniacs and the Gregorian Reform.* (Oxford University Press, A.D. 1970), pp. 32–34.]

[106] **Herimann of Toul:** was the immediate predecessor of Bruno as bishop. Known for his volatile temperament, he nevertheless played a formative role in Bruno's early career. Herimann's decision to entrust Bruno with leadership during the A.D. 1026 Italian campaign reflected Bruno's growing reputation for wisdom and composure—even as a young deacon.

[Robinson, Ian Stuart. *Authority and Resistance in the Investiture Contest: The Polemical Literature of the Late Eleventh Century.* (Manchester University Press, A.D. 1978), p. 21.]

too old to lead his contingent, he entrusted the command to Bruno, who was then a deacon. Though the military role was unexpected, it seems that Bruno had a natural affinity for soldiers and found some satisfaction in this new responsibility. During this period, Bruno's life took another turn. With Herimann's death, Bruno was elected to succeed him as Bishop of Toul. Conrad, seeing Bruno's potential for higher positions, was reluctant to allow him to accept such a small see. However, Bruno, preferring a life of humility and obscurity, persuaded Conrad to let him take on the position.

Consecrated in A.D. 1027, Bruno spent over twenty years administering the Diocese of Toul, facing numerous challenges such as famine and the constant threat of war, especially given the city's position as a frontier town. Bruno rose to the occasion, skillfully navigating both diplomacy and warfare. He forged a lasting peace between France and the Empire during his diplomatic mission to *Robert the Pious*,[107] a peace that endured even after the reigns of both

---

[107] **Robert the Pious:** (reigned A.D. 996–1031), was a deeply religious Capetian king who sought to strengthen the French monarchy while supporting ecclesiastical reform. His meeting with Bruno, later Pope Leo IX, during the negotiations that forged peace between France and the Empire, marked a significant diplomatic success. Robert's willingness to work with imperial envoys like Bruno underscored the king's preference for stability and reform across Christendom.

[Hallam, Elizabeth. *Capetian France: 987–1328.* (Longman, A.D. 1980), pp. 58–61.]

Conrad and Robert. Bruno also defended Toul against Eudes, Count

of Blois, a rebel against Conrad, and through his wisdom and

determination, he successfully integrated Burgundy into the Empire.

Amid these turbulent years, Bruno endured personal losses—

the deaths of his father, mother, and two brothers—yet he found

some solace in his love for music, where he excelled. Through it all,

he demonstrated an unshakeable commitment to both his spiritual

duties and the challenges of his time.

From Reluctant Candidate to Reforming Pontiff

In A.D. 1048, the death of the German *Pope Damasus II*[108]

prompted the Romans to request that *Emperor Henry III*[109] allow them

to elect a new pope. They considered either Halinard, Archbishop of

---

[108] **Pope Damasus II:** born Poppo of Brixen, served as pope for less than a month in A.D. 1048 before dying under mysterious circumstances, possibly due to malaria or foul play. He had been appointed by Emperor Henry III, making him the second of three German popes imposed by the emperor during his efforts to reform the papacy.

[Mann, Horace K. *The Lives of the Popes in the Early Middle Ages, Vol. 5.* (Kegan Paul, A.D. 1910), pp. 285–288.]

[109] **Emperor Henry III:** (reigned A.D. 1039–1056), was one of the most powerful Holy Roman Emperors of the Salian dynasty. He exercised unprecedented influence over the papacy, appointing a succession of German reform-minded popes. His choice of Bruno (later Leo IX) in A.D. 1048 was part of his broader campaign to purify and centralize the Church, and to combat simony and clerical incontinence.

[Robinson, I. S. *Henry IV of Germany, 1056–1106.* (Cambridge University Press, A.D. 2003), pp. 17–18.]

Lyons, or Bruno, both of whom had previously gained favor with the Romans during their pilgrimage to Rome. Henry III, however, immediately selected Bruno for the papacy. Despite the honor being thrust upon him, Bruno did everything he could to avoid it. Eventually, under the pressure of Henry, the Germans, and the Romans, he reluctantly agreed to travel to Rome. Bruno made it clear that he would accept the papacy only if freely elected by the Roman people.

Upon his arrival in Rome, Bruno, accompanied by *Hildebrand,*[110] presented himself to the people in the humble attire of a pilgrim—barefoot and unassuming, yet still striking in his appearance. The Romans, however, were resolute in their choice. With a unified voice, they declared that Bruno alone should be their pope. He was formally elected and took the name Leo IX, being solemnly enthroned on 12 February, A.D. 1049.

Before Pope Leo IX could begin the significant reforms to

---

[110] **Hildebrand:** the future Pope Gregory VII, was a young and rising reformer closely associated with the monastic ideals of Cluny. He accompanied Bruno on his journey to Rome in 1048, possibly helping orchestrate the public election that would legitimize Bruno's papacy. Hildebrand's early involvement in papal politics foreshadowed his later role in leading the Gregorian Reform and asserting papal supremacy.

[Cowdrey, H. E. J. *Pope Gregory VII, 1073–1085.* (Oxford University Press, A.D. 1998), pp. 5–6.]

the Church that were close to his heart, he first had to deal with the pressing issue of an attempted coup by the ex-Pope *Benedict IX,*[111] who sought to reclaim the papal throne. Once this threat was dealt with, Leo turned his attention to the dire state of the papal finances. Recognizing the need for change, he entrusted the management of the papacy's financial affairs to Hildebrand, whose reputation for effective reform was well-established. Through this move, Leo laid the groundwork for his papacy's focus on strengthening the Church and pursuing necessary reforms.

Champion of Church Renewal

Pope Leo IX's papacy marked the beginning of a profound transformation that would shape the Church for the next century, a movement later carried forward by his great successor, Gregory VII. One of Leo's first actions was to address two of the most pressing

---

[111] **Benedict IX:** born Theophylactus of Tusculum, is one of the most notorious figures in papal history. He held the papacy in three separate periods between A.D. 1032 and 1048 and was deposed or forced to resign each time. His final attempt to reclaim the papacy occurred after the death of Pope Damasus II in A.D. 1048. Benedict's repeated returns to power were supported by his powerful Roman aristocratic family, but his scandalous behavior—including charges of simony, violence, and immorality—made him a symbol of papal corruption. Leo IX's early efforts as pope were partially directed at quelling Benedict's ambitions and restoring legitimacy to the office.

     [Mann, Horace K. *The Lives of the Popes in the Early Middle Ages, Vol. 6.* (Kegan Paul, Trench, Trübner & Co., A.D. 1910), pp. 104–110.]

issues of the time: simony and clerical incontinence. In April, A.D. 1049, he convened a synod where he condemned these notorious evils, setting the stage for the sweeping reforms that would follow.

Leo's efforts to reform the Church were not confined to Rome. In May, A.D. 1049, he embarked on a series of journeys throughout Europe that earned him the title *Peregrinus Apostolicus*— the Apostolic Pilgrim. His first stop was Pavia, where he convened a council of reform, and then he traveled through Germany, reaching Cologne, where he met Emperor Henry III. Together, they brought peace to Lorraine by excommunicating the rebellious *Godfrey the Bearded*.[112]

Despite opposition from King Henry I of France, Leo continued his mission, traveling to Reims in France, where he held a significant synod. The synod saw participation from bishops and abbots from England, as well as a large and enthusiastic crowd of people from various regions, including Spain, Brittany, France,

---

[112] **Godfrey II:** was the Duke of Upper Lorraine—nicknamed *Godfrey the Bearded*— was a powerful noble who defied Emperor Henry III by rebelling against imperial authority in Lorraine. Pope Leo IX supported the emperor's efforts to maintain peace and discipline within the Empire and excommunicated Godfrey at the Council of Rheims in A.D. 1049 for his rebellion and military aggression.
    [Robinson, I. S. *The Papacy, 1073–1198: Continuity and Innovation.* (Cambridge University Press, A.D. 1990), p. 13.]

Ireland, and England. During this assembly, Leo excommunicated

the Archbishop of Compostela for assuming the title *Apostolicus*,[113]

reserved exclusively for the pope, and forbade the marriage between

William,[114] Duke of Normandy and Matilda of Flanders. The synod

also issued many reformative decrees, further solidifying Leo's

commitment to purifying the Church.

On his way back to Rome, Leo held another synod in Mainz,

where he continued to rally public opinion against the widespread

evils of the time. His travels were marked by widespread acclaim and

fervent support. It was during this journey that we first hear of the

---

[113] **Apostolicus:** is latin for "apostolic one"—was traditionally reserved for the Bishop of Rome (the pope) as the successor to the Apostle Peter. During the Council of Reims in A.D. 1049, Pope Leo IX excommunicated the Archbishop of Compostela (likely Cresconius or one of his immediate successors) for claiming this title illegitimately, which was seen as an affront to Roman primacy and papal authority.

> [Blumenthal, Uta-Renate. *The Investiture Controversy: Church and Monarchy from the Ninth to the Twelfth Century*. (University of Pennsylvania Press, A.D. 1988), p. 46.]

[114] **William the Conqueror:** (A.D. 1028–1087), originally Duke of Normandy, was a powerful Norman ruler who later became King of England after his victory at the Battle of Hastings in A.D. 1066. His marriage to Matilda of Flanders was initially forbidden by Pope Leo IX because the couple were closely related within prohibited degrees of consanguinity according to Church law at the time. Marriages between close relatives required papal dispensation, and Leo IX's synod forbade the union as part of broader efforts to enforce clerical discipline and Church laws on marriage and morality during the Gregorian Reform period. The marriage eventually took place with papal approval after formal dispensations were granted, underscoring the political and dynastic importance of their union.

> [Bates, David. *William the Conqueror*. (New Haven: Yale University Press, A.D. 2016), pp. 45–47.]

Golden Rose, a symbol of papal authority. As part of a privilege

granted by Leo to the Abbess of Woffenheim, she sent a golden rose

to Rome before Laetare Sunday, which was carried by the pope as a

symbol of his authority.

Before returning to Rome, Leo also discussed a plan with

Adalbert, Archbishop of Bremen, to establish a patriarchate for all

the Scandinavian countries, including Iceland and Greenland, with

the see based in Bremen. Although the scheme was never realized,

Leo did authorize the consecration of the first native bishop for

Iceland, further solidifying his role as a pivotal figure in the Church's

reform and expansion.

Struggles in Southern Italy and Beyond

In January, A.D. 1050, Pope Leo IX returned to Rome, but

his stay was brief as he quickly departed for Southern Italy,

responding to the urgent plight of its people who were being severely

oppressed by *the Normans*.[115] Despite Leo's efforts to address the

---

[115] **The Normans**: originally descended from Viking settlers in northern France (Normandy), the Normans became a formidable military force in Europe. By the mid-11th-century A.D., groups of Norman knights—initially serving as mercenaries in southern Italy—had established significant territorial control in the region, often at the expense of local rulers and populations.

situation, the Normans' cunning promises failed to alleviate the suffering of the people, and upon Leo's return to Rome after holding a council at Spoleto, the oppression continued unabated.

During the annual Paschal synod that Leo typically held in Rome, he condemned the heresy of *Berengarius of Tours*,[116] a condemnation he reiterated months later in Vercelli. As A.D. 1050 drew to a close, Leo embarked on his second transalpine journey. His first destination was Toul, where he solemnly translated the relics of Gerard, bishop of the city, whom he had recently canonized. He then traveled to Germany to meet with *Emperor Henry the Black*.[117] This meeting had notable consequences, one of which was the emperor

---

[Loud, G.A. *The Age of Robert Guiscard: Southern Italy and the Norman Conquest*. (London: Longman, A.D. 2000), pp. 3–12]

[116] **Berengarius of Tours:** (A.D. 999–1088), was a French cleric whose controversial views on the Eucharist sparked major theological conflict. He rejected the doctrine of transubstantiation—the belief that the bread and wine become the actual body and blood of Christ during the Mass—arguing instead for a more symbolic or spiritual presence. His teachings were condemned multiple times, including by Pope Leo IX at the A.D. 1050 synod in Rome and again at the Synod of Vercelli later that year.

[Macy, Gary. *The Theologies of the Eucharist in the Early Scholastic Period* (Oxford: Oxford University Press, A.D. 1984), 38–42]

[117] **Emperor Henry III:** (reigned A.D. 1039–1056), known as "the Black" (Latin: *Heinricus Niger*), likely earned the epithet due to his dark hair or complexion—a distinguishing feature in contemporary accounts. A devout and forceful ruler of the Holy Roman Empire, Henry supported ecclesiastical reform and directly intervened in papal affairs, appointing several popes including Leo IX. His close collaboration with the reform papacy marked a high point in imperial-papal relations.

[Robinson, I.S. *Henry IV of Germany, 1056–1106*. (Cambridge: Cambridge University Press, A.D. 2003), pp. 3–6]

compelling Hunfrid, Archbishop of Ravenna, to cease acting as an independent ruler and to submit to papal authority.

Returning to Rome, Leo convened another Paschal synod in April, A.D. 1051 before heading to Benevento (southern Italy) in July. The Beneventans, besieged by enemies, concluded that the only path to peace was to place themselves under papal protection. Leo was received into the city with great honor. While in the region, he made further attempts to curb the excesses of the Normans. However, these efforts were undermined by the native Lombards, who, driven by both folly and malice, massacred several Normans in Apulia. Realizing that further action against the surviving, enraged Normans was futile, Leo retraced his steps back to Rome in A.D. 1051.

Struggles Against the Normans

The Norman question remained a constant concern for Pope Leo IX throughout his papacy. The people of Southern Italy, continually oppressed by the Normans, never ceased to implore the pope for help. The Greeks, fearing complete expulsion from the peninsula, also begged for Leo's assistance in confronting the common enemy. Pressed on all sides, Leo sought help from various quarters. However, after his efforts to rally support proved unsuccessful, he once again turned to direct mediation in A.D. 1052, but his attempts were met with failure.

Growing increasingly convinced that a military response was inevitable, Leo prepared to take more drastic measures. At this point, an embassy from the Hungarians arrived, requesting the pope's intervention to bring peace between them and Emperor Henry. Leo, confident that his involvement would bring success, crossed the Alps once more. Unfortunately, Henry rejected the terms proposed by the pope, leading to the failure of Leo's peace mission with the Hungarians. Although initially offering to support Leo with a German force to fight the Normans, Henry later withdrew his promise. As a result, Leo returned to Italy with only a few German troops, raised by his relatives, in A.D. 1053.

Upon returning to Rome in March A.D. 1053, Leo found the situation in Southern Italy even more dire. In response, he mustered what forces he could from the Italian princes and declared war on the Normans. He aimed to join forces with the Greek general, but the Normans defeated both the Greeks and the pope's army at Civitella in southern Italy in June, A.D. 1053. After the battle, Leo surrendered to the Normans, who treated him with great respect and declared themselves his soldiers.

Patriarch Michael Caerularius

After his defeat at Civitella, Pope Leo IX withdrew to Benevento, deeply troubled and heartbroken. The deaths of his soldiers haunted him, and his attention turned to the growing tensions with *Michael Caerularius,*[118] the ambitious Patriarch of Constantinople. Caerularius had long harbored ambitions to have no superior in either the Church or the State. As early as A.D. 1042, he had removed the pope's name from the *sacred diptychs,*[119] and his attacks on the Latin Church escalated. He criticized the Latin practice of using unleavened bread (*azymes*) in the Mass and, in a particularly

---

[118] **Michael Caerularius:** (also spelled Cerularius), served as Patriarch of Constantinople from A.D. 1043 to 1059. His tenure was marked by increasing hostility toward the Latin Church, culminating in the events of the East–West Schism of A.D. 1054. He was especially noted for opposing Latin liturgical practices and asserting Constantinople's ecclesiastical independence from Rome.
   [Runciman, Steven. *The Eastern Schism.* (Oxford: Clarendon Press, A.D. 1955), pp. 41–44.]

[119] **Sacred diptychs:** were liturgical lists commemorating the living and dead, especially church leaders, read during the Divine Liturgy. The removal of the pope's name from the diptychs by Michael Caerularius was a formal and symbolic rejection of communion with Rome.
   [Dvornik, Francis. *Byzantium and the Roman Primacy.* (New York: Fordham University Press, A.D. 1966), p. 107.]

harsh move, closed Latin churches in Constantinople.

In response to these provocations, Pope Leo addressed Michael with a strong letter in September, A.D. 1053 and began studying Greek to better understand the theological issues at hand. While Leo faced pressure from the Normans in the West, Michael took advantage of the pope's difficulties to further his own agenda. However, the Greek Emperor, Constantine, recognized that the success of the Normans in Southern Italy threatened his own position. As a result, he pressured Caerularius to be more respectful toward the pope.

In early A.D. 1054, conciliatory letters were sent by both Emperor Constantine and Patriarch Caerularius to Leo, with the hope of mending relations. Leo responded to these letters in January, A.D. 1054, reprimanding Caerularius for his arrogance. To deliver these letters, Leo sent two distinguished cardinals, Humbert and Frederick, on an important mission to Constantinople. However, Pope Leo IX passed away before the results of their mission reached Rome.

On 16 July, A.D. 1054, the two cardinals, Humbert and Frederick, issued the excommunication of Michael Caerularius, marking the formal split between the Eastern and Western Churches. The East was now definitively severed from the body of the Catholic Church, a momentous event in Christian history known as the East-West Schism.

England and His Final Days

Pope Leo IX had significant relations with England during his pontificate, particularly with its saintly *King Edward the Confessor*.[120] When King Edward made a vow to undertake a pilgrimage to Rome, Pope Leo dispensed him from this vow, on the condition that the king provide alms to the poor and endow a monastery in honor of St. Peter. Additionally, Leo authorized the transfer of the See of Crediton to Exeter and took firm action against the consecration of the unworthy Abbot of Abingdon, Spearhafor, as Bishop of London. Throughout the difficulties faced by Archbishop *Robert of Jumièges*[121]

---

[120] **Edward the Confessor:** (reigned A.D. 1042–1066) was known for his piety and is considered one of the last Anglo-Saxon kings of England. His vow to go on pilgrimage to Rome was dispensed by Pope Leo IX, who instead directed him to perform charitable and ecclesiastical works.
  [Barlow, Frank. *Edward the Confessor.* (Berkeley: University of California Press, A.D. 1970), pp. 123–126.]

[121] **Robert of Jumièges:** a Norman cleric, was appointed Archbishop of Canterbury in A.D. 1051. He was opposed by the powerful Earl Godwin, and ultimately fled England. Pope Leo IX supported Robert and legitimized his claim by sending him the pallium.

of Canterbury, particularly his struggles with the family of *Earl*

Godwin,[122] Pope Leo supported him by sending him the pallium and

condemning Stigand, the usurper of the Canterbury see.

It is also believed that *King Macbeth of Scotland,*[123] who had

been involved in the murder of *King Duncan,*[124] may have visited

Rome during Leo's pontificate. It is speculated that Macbeth may

have sought spiritual guidance from the pope, thus adding another

dimension to Leo's far-reaching influence.

However, after the defeat at Civitella, Leo IX never fully

recovered his spirits. His health began to decline, and in March, A.D.

1054, he was struck by a mortal illness. Despite his failing health, he

---

[Mason, Emma. *House of Godwin: The History of a Dynasty.* (London: Hambledon and London, A.D. 2004), pp. 88–91.]

[122] **Earl Godwin of Wessex:** was one of the most powerful nobles in England during Edward's reign and a key opponent of Norman influence, especially Robert of Jumièges. His conflict with the king culminated in his temporary exile in A.D. 1051.

[Walker, Ian. *Harold: The Last Anglo-Saxon King.* (Stroud: Sutton Publishing, A.D. 1997), pp. 18–22.]

[123] **King Macbeth of Scotland:** (reigned A.D. 1040–1057), who seized the throne after killing King Duncan, is believed by some sources to have made a pilgrimage to Rome in A.D. 1050. Though the motive is uncertain, it may have involved penance or a show of royal legitimacy.

[Broun, Dauvit. *"Macbeth,"* in *Oxford Dictionary of National Biography,* ed. H.C.G. Matthew and Brian Harrison. (Oxford: Oxford University Press, A.D. 2004).]

[124] **King Duncan I of Scotland:** (reigned A.D. 1034–1040), was killed by Macbeth in battle, an event that later inspired Shakespeare's dramatization. Duncan's death marked a shift in Scottish royal succession.

[Duncan, A.A.M. *The Kingship of the Scots: Succession and Independence 842–1292.* (Edinburgh: Edinburgh University Press, A.D. 2002), p. 43.]

had himself transported back to Rome, where he died a peaceful and edifying death. His life and death were marked by miracles, both during his lifetime and after his passing. Pope Leo IX was buried in St. Peter's Basilica, and his sanctity was recognized by the Roman Martyrology, securing his legacy as a revered figure in the Church.

Chapter X

Pope Leo X (A.D. 1513-1521)

Early Life of Pope Leo X

Five centuries passed before another Pope Leo was elected to

the papacy, and his life was as remarkable as his papacy would later

be. Giovanni de' Medici, who would become Pope Leo X, was born

on December 11, A.D. 1475, in Florence. He was the second son of

the renowned *Lorenzo de' Medici*[125] his wife, *Clarice Orsini.*[126] From a

---

[125] **Lorenzo de' Medici:** (A.D. 1449–1492), known as "the Magnificent," was the de facto ruler of Florence and one of the most influential patrons of Renaissance art and culture. As head of the Medici family, he used his wealth and influence to maintain stability in Florence and to support a flourishing of artistic and intellectual life.

> [Hibbert, Christopher. *The House of Medici: Its Rise and Fall.* (New York: William Morrow, A.D. 1975), pp. 163–180]

[126] **Clarice Orsini:** (A.D. 1453–1488), was a Roman noblewoman from the powerful Orsini family. Her marriage to Lorenzo de' Medici in A.D. 1469 was politically strategic, cementing ties between Florence and Rome. Though not as culturally engaged as her husband, she was respected for her piety and fulfilled her duties as a Medici matriarch.

> [Kent, Dale. *Lorenzo de' Medici and the Art of Magnificence.* (Baltimore: Johns Hopkins University Press, A.D. 2004), pp. 95–97]

young age, Giovanni's path seemed set for the Church, a future his family eagerly anticipated.

In A.D. 1482, at just seven years old, Giovanni received the *tonsure,*[127] marking his formal entry into ecclesiastical life. By the age of eight, he was appointed Abbot of Font Douce in the French Diocese of Saintes and later appointed *Apostolic Prothonotary*[128] by Pope Sixtus IV in A.D. 1483. The Medici family, with its extensive influence, secured a wealth of benefices for Giovanni, and he soon became the holder of prestigious positions such as the Abbey of Passignano in A.D. 1484 and Monte Cassino in A.D. 1486.

The pressure from his father, Lorenzo, to secure Giovanni's prominence in the Church led Pope Innocent VIII to make the young boy a cardinal at the tender age of 13 in A.D. 1489. This

---

[127] **Tonsure:** was the ceremonial cutting or shaving of hair from the scalp of clerics as a symbol of religious devotion and entrance into ecclesiastical life. In the Latin Church, it marked the beginning of a clerical career and was typically administered to boys or young men destined for the priesthood.

[Jungmann, Joseph A. *The Early Liturgy to the Time of Gregory the Great, trans. Francis A. Brunner.* (Notre Dame, IN: University of Notre Dame Press, A.D. 1959), pp. 74–76.]

[128] **Apostolic Prothonotary:** (Latin: *Protonotarius Apostolicus*), is a senior administrative official in the papal curia. In the Renaissance, the title denoted a member of a college of prelates responsible for drafting and authenticating significant papal documents. It was often granted as an honorific to promising young clerics of noble background.

[Oakley, Francis. *The Western Church in the Later Middle Ages.* (Ithaca: Cornell University Press, A.D. 1979), pp. 145–146.]

promotion came with the stipulation that Giovanni would forgo the ceremonial insignia and privileges of his office for three years, allowing him to focus on his studies. During this time, he received an education that would shape his future—immersing himself in the works of the era's finest humanists, including Angelo Poliziano, Marsilio Ficino, and Bernardo Dovizi, who would later become Cardinal Bibbiena.

From A.D. 1489 to 1491, Giovanni studied theology and canon law at the University of Pisa, under the tutelage of prominent scholars Filippo Decio and Bartolomeo Sozzini. After completing his studies, he was formally invested with the cardinalate on 9 March, A.D. 1492, in Fiesole. Upon his arrival in Rome on 22 March, he was ceremoniously received by Pope Innocent VIII and the College of Cardinals. Despite his youth, Giovanni impressed the Romans with his maturity, his conduct surpassing what might have been expected from someone of his age.

In a personal letter to his son, Lorenzo the Magnificent shared wise counsel, urging Giovanni to be honorable, virtuous, and exemplary in his conduct, especially within the College of Cardinals, which at the time lacked moral integrity. This letter reflected

Lorenzo's own growing wisdom in his final years and served as a guiding influence for Giovanni as he navigated the complex world of the papacy.

Tumultuous Years

In the very next month following the death of his father, Lorenzo the Magnificent, Giovanni de' Medici was called back to Florence. The family's political fortunes had taken a dramatic turn, and Giovanni was thrust into the complexities of his father's legacy. However, his return to Rome for the papal election in A.D. 1492 brought an outcome that he strongly opposed: the elevation of *Pope Alexander VI*,[129] a figure whom Giovanni deemed unworthy of the papacy. With this disappointing result, Giovanni withdrew to Florence, where he would remain until the expulsion of the Medici family in A.D. 1494.

---

[129] **Pope Alexander VI:** born Rodrigo Borgia, was elected in A.D. 1492 amid significant controversy and political intrigue. His papacy became notorious for nepotism and corruption, which drew sharp criticism from contemporaries like Giovanni de' Medici, who viewed Alexander VI as unworthy of the papal office. This contentious election influenced the political dynamics in Florence and Italy at large during the early A.D. 1490s.

[Gregorovius, Ferdinand. *The History of the City of Rome in the Middle Ages, Vol. 5.* (London: George Bell & Sons, A.D. 1906), pp. 372–380]

Pope Leo X

During these years in Florence, Giovanni faced a period of political turmoil and personal struggle. Forced into exile after the Medici were ousted, he fled the city in the humble garb of a Franciscan monk, a symbol of both his forced departure and the temporary collapse of his family's political influence. He made several attempts to restore the supremacy of the Medici family but, despite his best efforts, these attempts proved fruitless. Giovanni's personal life during this period was marked by a deep engagement with the arts and letters, leading him to embrace a more literary and artistic lifestyle. Yet, despite his patronage of the arts and his liberal generosity, Giovanni's poor financial management often left him in distressing circumstances. His lack of financial acumen remained a challenge throughout his life.

Although his lifestyle appeared worldly and indulgent, Giovanni remained a model of dignity, propriety, and moral conduct—qualities that distinguished him from many of his peers in the College of Cardinals. His personal integrity shone through in contrast to the indulgences and excesses that plagued the Church during this time.

The Legacy of Pope Leo

Towards the end of the pontificate of *Pope Julius II*[130] (A.D.
1503-1513), Giovanni's fortunes began to change. With Julius II
gravely ill in August, A.D. 1511, Giovanni, ever ambitious, began to
look toward the papacy. In October of that year, he was appointed
papal legate to Bologna and Romagna, a move that rekindled his
hopes of restoring his family's power and influence, particularly in
Florence. The Florentines, who had sided with the *schismatic Pisans,*[131]
found themselves at odds with the papacy. In response, Pope Julius
II supported Giovanni and the Medici family.

However, Giovanni's journey was far from smooth. In A.D.
1512, the Spanish and papal forces, with Giovanni among them,
suffered a decisive defeat at *the Battle of Ravenna*[132] at the hands of the

---

[130] **Pope Julius II:** pontiff from A.D. 1503 to 1513, was a decisive and militaristic
pope who sought to strengthen the temporal power of the papacy in Italy. Even as
his health declined in A.D. 1511, he actively maneuvered politically, including
appointing Giovanni de' Medici as papal legate to consolidate papal influence in
key regions like Bologna and Romagna.
   [Pastor, Ludwig von. *The History of the Popes, From the Close of the Middle
   Ages, Vol. 5: Julius II.* (London: Kegan Paul, Trench, Trübner & Co., A.D.
   1912), pp. 75–85.]
[131] **Schismatic Pisans:** were a faction in Pisa that opposed papal authority during
the early-16th-century A.D., aligning themselves against the papacy and the Medici-
aligned Florentines. Their defiance brought them into direct conflict with Pope
Julius II, who supported the Medici efforts to reassert control over Florence and its
environs.
   [Hibbert, Christopher. *The House of Medici: Its Rise and Fall.* (New York:
   William Morrow & Co., A.D. 1974), pp. 192–195.]
[132] **The Battle of Ravenna:** fought on 11 April, A.D. 1512, was a significant
conflict during the War of the League of Cambrai. Despite tactical French victory

French. Giovanni was captured and faced the prospect of being taken to France as a prisoner. Yet, fate intervened. The French, despite their victory, soon lost all their territorial holdings in Italy, and Giovanni managed to escape his captivity, narrowly avoiding a grim fate.

In September A.D. 1512, the Medici were once again firmly in control of Florence, and Giovanni's family's restored supremacy marked the beginning of an even greater rise. This unexpected reversal of fortune would soon set the stage for Giovanni's ascent to even higher honors, culminating in his eventual election to the papacy as Pope Leo X.

Pontiff of Patronage

On 11 March 1513, Giovanni de' Medici, at the age of thirty-eight, ascended to the papacy, following the death of Julius II on 21 February. His election was a quiet affair, with Giovanni receiving only a single vote in the first scrutiny. His supporters, the younger

---

against the combined Spanish and papal forces, the battle resulted in heavy casualties on both sides. Giovanni de' Medici fought alongside the papal troops and was captured by the French. Though taken prisoner, he was later released under circumstances that preserved his influence.
[Oman, Charles. *A History of the Art of War in the Sixteenth Century*. (London: Methuen & Co., A.D. 1937), pp. 201–205]

cardinals, held back his candidacy until the right moment, and when his election finally came, it was met with approval even in France. However, there was a degree of skepticism surrounding whether the youthful pope would be able to shoulder the immense responsibilities of the papacy. Many placed high hopes in him—politicians who saw him as pliable, scholars and artists who had already received his patronage, and theologians who longed for much-needed church reforms under a more benevolent ruler.

Unfortunately, Pope Leo X would largely fulfill the expectations of the artists, literati, and pleasure-seeking courtiers who viewed the papal court as a center of entertainment rather than serious governance. Leo's personal appearance is immortalized in Raphael's famous painting at the Pitti Gallery in Florence, where he is shown with Cardinals Medici and Rossi. Though not an imposing figure, Leo's corpulence and effeminate countenance are evident in the painting, with his shiny face, weak eyes, and sluggish movements, often wiping sweat from his brow during ecclesiastical functions. However, his unpleasant physical appearance was softened by his agreeable voice, elegant speech, and gracious manner. It is said that after his election, he remarked, "Let us enjoy the papacy since God has given it to us,"[133] a sentiment that, though recorded by a Venetian ambassador, aptly reflects the pope's pleasure-seeking nature.

Pope Leo X was largely indifferent to the challenges and dangers facing the papacy, instead indulging in a life of amusement and lavish entertainments. His love of pleasure was characteristic of the Medici family. Music, theatre, art, and poetry all held a strong appeal for him, much like any pampered aristocrat of his time. Although he led a temperate personal lifestyle, he was a frequent host of grand banquets and lavish celebrations filled with revelry and drinking. His passion for hunting, which he carried out on an extensive scale each year, further demonstrated his indulgent nature. From an early age, Leo was a devoted lover of music, surrounding himself with the best musicians and listening to improvisations at his dinner table. Surprisingly, despite his lofty position and artistic tastes, he also had a fondness for the crude humor of buffoons, enjoying their absurd jokes and extravagant appetites.

Leo's court was a stage for extravagant entertainments, with masques, music, and theatrical performances becoming fixtures of his

---

[133] Lilly, William Samuel. *The Claims of Christianity*. (London: Chapman & Hall, A.D. 1894), p. 127.

papacy, especially during the Carnival. Even in the turbulent year of

A.D. 1520, he participated in particularly opulent festivities. The

papal palace became akin to a theatre, and Leo did not shy away from

attending plays that were deemed morally questionable, such as

Bibbiena's *Calendra*[134] and Ariosto's *Suppositi.*[135] His contemporaries

often praised his infectious good humor, a trait he maintained even in

the face of adversity. Cheerful and good-natured, he believed in the

value of happiness and sought to spread joy to others.

Leo's generosity was one of his most admirable qualities. A

patron of the arts and an advocate for his fellow Florentines, he

welcomed his relatives to Rome, where they seized official positions.

He was equally generous to the artists, poets, and petitioners who

sought his favor. His largesse was sincere, and his giving was not

---

[134] **Calandra:** (A.D. 1513), one of the earliest Italian prose comedies, was performed at Pope Leo X's court despite its morally ambiguous content. The play features themes of cross-dressing, sexual mischief, and deception—centered on a young man disguising himself as a woman to gain access to a noble household. These elements, while entertaining to humanist audiences, were seen by critics as subversive to traditional Christian values of modesty and decorum.

  [Herrick, Marvin T. *Italian Comedy in the Renaissance.* (Urbana: University of Illinois Press, A.D. 1960), pp. 103–104.]

[135] **Suppositi:** (A.D. 1509), also staged for Leo X, similarly drew criticism for its irreverent themes. The play involves mistaken identity, imposture, and romantic deception, often mocking parental authority and social order. Though derived from Roman comedic models, its open treatment of illicit love and trickery led many contemporaries—especially within the Church—to view it as morally suspect.

  [Hankins, James. *Virtue Politics: Soulcraft and Statecraft in Renaissance Italy.* (Cambridge, MA: Harvard University Press, A.D. 2019), p. 430.]

motivated by vanity but by genuine compassion. He gave freely, and his charity was extensive. Convents, hospitals, discharged soldiers, students, exiles, the sick, and the downtrodden all found a benefactor in Leo. Each year, over 6,000 ducats were distributed in alms, demonstrating the pope's deep commitment to charitable acts and social welfare.

Despite the criticisms of his indulgent lifestyle, Pope Leo X's reign was a period of remarkable cultural flourishing, thanks in large part to his unwavering support of the arts. Yet, his inability or unwillingness to confront the more pressing spiritual and political crises of his time would leave a complex legacy. While he excelled as a patron and a figure of leisure, his pontificate was also marked by the growing tensions that would eventually erupt in the *Protestant Revolt*.[136]

---

[136] **Protestant Revolt:** is a term that has traditionally been employed by Catholic historians to characterize the early-16th-century A.D. movement initiated by Martin Luther and other reformers as a heretical rupture in the unity of the Church. This designation emphasizes the movement's roots in protest (*protestatio*) and rebellion against ecclesiastical authority. In contrast, later Protestant and Whig historians reinterpreted this period as the "Reformation," portraying it as a positive and inevitable advance toward religious and political liberty—an emblematic term within the framework of Whig history.

[MacCulloch, Diarmaid. *The Reformation: A History*. (Penguin Books, A.D. 2004).]

Financial Irresponsibility

The financial legacy of Pope Leo X was marked by profound mismanagement and unrestrained spending, which quickly squandered the substantial treasure left by his predecessor, Julius II. By the spring of A.D. 1515, the papal treasury had been entirely depleted, and Leo never succeeded in recovering from his financial troubles. In his desperation, he resorted to dubious and unethical methods to raise funds, including the sale of offices and dignities, some of which were among the highest positions in the Church. Jubilees and indulgences, once spiritual in nature, were increasingly reduced to mere financial transactions, but despite these efforts, the treasury remained empty.

Leo's papal income, which amounted to between 500,000 and 600,000 ducats, was hardly sufficient to cover the lavish expenditures of his papacy. The papal household, which had been maintained on 48,000 ducats under Julius II, now cost double that amount. Over the course of his pontificate, Leo spent approximately four and a half million ducats, leaving behind a debt of 400,000 ducats. His unexpected death plunged his creditors into financial ruin, and a biting lampoon proclaimed that "Leo X had consumed three pontificates: the treasure of Julius II, the revenues of his own reign, and those of his successor."[137]

Despite his financial failures, it is important to acknowledge the more positive aspects of Leo's character and reign. He was a highly cultivated man, with an appreciation for all that was beautiful. A polished orator and an accomplished writer, Leo possessed a sharp memory and sound judgment, which contributed to his dignified and majestic manner. Even those who were critical of him recognized his intellectual abilities and refined sensibilities. Leo's love for the arts and his patronage of artists and scholars are well-documented, and his papacy is often regarded as a golden age for the Italian Renaissance.

In matters of personal piety, Leo was generally considered a devout man, despite the shortcomings in his spiritual life. He adhered to the daily rituals of the Church, attending Mass and reading his Breviary each day, while also fasting three times a week. His devotion, however, was not deeply spiritual in nature, and there is no record of any expressions of doubt or skepticism on his part. The

---

[137] Schaff, *History of the Christian Church*, *Vol. 6*. (the A.D. 1910 Charles Scribner's Sons edition), pp. 192–193.]

infamous quote, "How much we and our family have profited by the legend of Christ, is sufficiently evident to all ages," attributed to Leo, is widely regarded as a later fabrication by John Bale, an English Carmelite who lived long after the pope's death. As such, it should not be used to tarnish Leo's reputation unfairly.

Even during his papacy, Leo managed to maintain the irreproachable reputation he had built as a cardinal. His private life was marked by integrity, and he was respected for his dignified conduct. However, his reign was a striking example of the complex interplay of good and bad traits. On one hand, Leo X was a refined, intellectual, and well-meaning individual, while on the other, he was a financially reckless leader whose extravagance ultimately led to the financial ruin of the papacy. His pontificate serves as a reminder of the challenges faced by a pope who sought to balance worldly indulgence with spiritual duties.

Flourishing in Art, Literature, and Science

Pope Leo X's papacy is largely celebrated for its remarkable patronage of literature, science, and art, which transformed Rome into the undisputed center of the literary world during the early-16th-century A.D. His reign coincided with the high point of the Renaissance, and under his guidance, the Eternal City became a haven for scholars, poets, and artists.

One of the most notable groups to flourish during Leo's papacy was the poets. Few princes in history have been as lauded in verse as Leo X, whose name was frequently immortalized in the works of the poets he supported. The pope was not only generous in awarding gifts, titles, and positions to established poets and scholars but also extended his patronage to lesser talents, even rewarding poetasters and jesters with similar favors. Among the most esteemed figures in Leo's literary circle were the papal secretaries Pietro Bembo and Jacopo Sadoleto, both of whom were celebrated poets and prose writers.

Bembo, known for his polished wit, was an influential figure in the literary world. His letters, written in the classical *Ciceronian style,*[138] were highly regarded and reflected his wide-ranging intellectual

---

[138] **Ciceronian style:** refers to a form of Latin prose modeled after the writings of Marcus Tullius Cicero, characterized by balanced periods, rhythmic structure, clarity, and elegance. Renaissance humanists like Pietro Bembo revived this style to emulate classical Latin's rhetorical sophistication and purity.

[Grafton, Anthony and Williams, Megan. *Rome Reborn: The Vatican Library and Renaissance Culture.* (Harvard University Press, A.D. 2009), p. 57.]

interactions with the great minds of his time. Bembo's scholarly

endeavors included preparing a critical edition of Dante's works and

assembling an impressive collection of manuscripts, books, and

works of art. Despite his contributions to literature, Bembo's lifestyle

was not entirely in line with the lofty position he held as papal notary

and count palatine. He was known for his worldly pleasures and

indulgences, which contrasted with the ascetic nature of his office.

In contrast, Sadoleto represented a more virtuous figure. A

model priest, Sadoleto was admired for his pure and spotless life. He

embodied a synthesis of ancient and modern culture and was a

passionate advocate for antiquity. Like Bembo, Sadoleto's elegance

and refinement made him a key figure in the literary world, but he

distinguished himself through his moral integrity and devotion to his

religious duties.

The literary scene in Rome also saw the rise of many other

notable poets. Marco Girolamo Vida, for example, composed the

highly regarded epic poem *Christiade* and was celebrated as the

"Christian Virgil" by his contemporaries. Another prominent figure

was Sannazaro, whose epic poem on the birth of Christ set a new

standard for stylistic excellence. Other poets, such as the Carmelite

Pope Leo X

Spagnolo Mantovano, whose *Calendar of Feasts* combined Christian themes with classical references, and Ferreri, who reimagined the Breviary hymns with pagan imagery, also contributed to the vibrant literary culture of the period.

In total, more than a hundred poets flourished in Rome during Leo X's papacy. While many of these poets have faded into obscurity, their collective impact on the cultural development of Renaissance Rome was undeniable. A lampoon from A.D. 1521 humorously claimed that the number of poets in Rome exceeded the stars in the sky, highlighting the sheer volume of literary activity under Leo's patronage. Although most of these poets have been forgotten by history, the flourishing of art, literature, and intellectual life during Leo X's reign remains a significant chapter in the story of the Renaissance.

Leo X's contributions to the arts were not limited to literature. His enthusiastic support for artists, musicians, and scholars left a lasting legacy that helped shape the cultural and intellectual climate of the time. However, it was his role in transforming Rome into a vibrant hub for Renaissance thought and creativity that solidified his place in history as one of the great patrons of the arts.

Impact on Literature, Art, and Science

Pope Leo X's papacy was marked by his notable, albeit sometimes overrated, contributions to literature, science, and art, establishing a legacy that had a profound effect on the cultural development of the West. While his patronage was wide-ranging, not all efforts were as successful or as sustained as his more celebrated contributions to the arts.

In literature, Leo X's support was far-reaching, although its impact was not always profound. The Italian poets of the time were prolific, yet few produced truly remarkable works. Among them, Gian Giorgio Trissino wrote a tragedy, *Sophonisba*, and an epic, *L'Italia liberata dai Gothi*, but neither gained much success despite the beauty of his language and earnest intent. A relative of the pope, Rucellai, wrote a widely praised didactic poem on bees, though his reputation was largely based on a lesser tragedy, *Rosmonda*. The famed improvisatore Tebaldeo, who wrote in both Latin and Italian, was another figure of note during this period. However, Leo X's harsh treatment of Ludovico Ariosto, another major figure in Renaissance literature, stands out as a blemish on his literary patronage. Despite these shortcomings, Leo did provide significant encouragement to the study of ancient texts, particularly through the work of Manetti, whose *Roman Topographical Inscriptions* was the first comprehensive collection published in A.D. 1521, heralding a new era in archaeology. This was complemented by the contributions of scholars like Fulvio, Castiglione, and Raphael, who planned a survey of ancient Rome, although Raphael's early death interrupted the project.

Leo also gave considerable support to Greek studies. Aldus Manutius, a Venetian publisher, became one of Leo's protégés and was instrumental in making Greek classics more widely accessible. Leo invited the Greek scholars Andreas Johannes Lascaris and Musurus to Rome, where they founded the *Medicean Academy,*[139] further promoting Greek culture and learning in the city. Despite these initiatives, Leo's attempts to increase the treasures of the Vatican Library, including sending emissaries as far as Scandinavia

---

[139] **Medicean Academy:** Pope Leo X invited the Greek scholars Johannes Lascaris and Marcus Musurus to Rome, where they founded the Medicean Academy, promoting Greek culture and classical learning in the city during the early-16th-century A.D. This institution helped revive the study of Greek classics and contributed to the flourishing of humanism under Leo's patronage.
[Löffler, K. *Pope Leo X. In The Catholic Encyclopedia, Vol. 9.* (New York: Charles Scribner's Sons, A.D. 1910), p. 692.]

and the Orient, yielded limited results. *The Roman university,*[140] which had been in decline, was reformed during his reign but did not enjoy lasting prosperity. Overall, as a literary patron, Leo X's efforts were hampered by insufficient funds and a lack of thoroughness in distributing his favors, leaving him with a legacy more of ambition than of true achievement.

Leo's greatest influence, however, came through his patronage of the visual arts, particularly painting. Under his patronage, the great Raphael reached the height of his career. Raphael had arrived in Rome in A.D. 1508, summoned by Pope Julius II, and remained there until his death in A.D. 1520. Leo's support was pivotal in allowing Raphael to produce some of his most important works. Among these was the completion of the Vatican Stanze, which had been begun under Julius II, and the creation of the tapestries for the Sistine Chapel, including the magnificent *St. Peter's Miraculous Draught of Fishes* and *St. Paul Preaching in Athens.* Leo also

---

[140] **The Roman University**: also known as the Sapienza University of Rome—had been established centuries earlier but experienced a decline by the late-15th-and early-16th-centuries A.D. due to political instability and lack of sustained support. When Pope Leo X became pontiff (A.D. 1513–1521), he sought to revive this important center of learning as part of his broader patronage of the arts and scholarship.

> [Burke, Peter. *The Renaissance and the University: Education, Humanism, and the Arts.* (Cambridge University Press, A.D. 1999), pp. 112–115.]

entrusted Raphael with the design and decoration of the Vatican Loggia, executed by Raphael's pupils under his guidance. Some of Raphael's finest works, including the *Sistine Madonna* and the *Transfiguration*, were completed under Leo's watch. In these paintings, Raphael's mastery of the human form and his ability to elevate religious themes to the level of high art reached their zenith, ensuring his legacy as one of the greatest artists in history.

However, sculpture under Leo X experienced a marked decline. Although Michelangelo offered his services, his work on the marble façade for the church of San Lorenzo in Florence was left unfinished, a testament to the challenges the pope faced in executing large-scale artistic projects. On the other hand, Leo gave significant attention to the decorative and industrial arts, encouraging the minor arts and craftsmanship, and this contributed to the flourishing of decorative carving and other applied arts.

Perhaps the most difficult and ongoing task that Leo X inherited from Julius II was the continuation of St. Peter's Basilica. The renowned architect Bramante had been chief architect until his death in A.D. 1514, and Raphael succeeded him in this role. However, due to financial constraints, Raphael's work on St. Peter's was limited, and the grandeur of the project was not fully realized during his brief tenure.

In conclusion, Leo X's papacy marked a period of cultural stimulation, particularly in the fields of art and literature. Although his contributions to literature were not as lasting or as significant as his influence on the visual arts, he played an essential role in supporting the Renaissance's intellectual and artistic flourishing. His most enduring legacy is undoubtedly his patronage of Raphael, whose work remains a monumental achievement in the history of art. While his financial imprudence and lack of long-term vision hindered some of his scholarly and intellectual efforts, Leo X's role as a patron of the arts solidified his place in history as one of the key figures in the cultural development of the Renaissance.

Political and Religious Events

While Pope Leo X's papacy is often remembered for its cultural achievements, the political and religious aspects of his reign present a more complex and often troubled picture. His well-known inclination toward peace, combined with the delicate political situation of his time, led to a series of challenges and compromises that ultimately marred his pontificate.

Leo X inherited a difficult political situation, especially due to the continuing conflict between France and Italy. France, still stung by its defeat in A.D. 1512, sought to avenge its loss and regain control of Milan. This ambition led to France forming an alliance with Venice, which prompted *Emperor Maximilian*,[141] Spain, and England to counteract this alliance by forming *the Holy League*[142] in A.D. 1513. Initially, Leo hoped to maintain neutrality in this volatile conflict, but such a stance would have isolated the Papal States. Faced with the pressure of aligning with one side, Leo decided to follow the policies of his predecessors and oppose France, but he did so cautiously, avoiding harsh actions.

---

[141] **Emperor Maximilian I:** was Holy Roman Emperor from A.D. 1493 to 1519. He played a pivotal role in the Italian Wars by forming the Holy League in A.D. 1513. This alliance—comprising the Holy Roman Empire, Spain, and England—was designed to counteract the Franco-Venetian alliance and to maintain Habsburg and papal influence in Italy.

> [Chambers, David. *The Imperial Age of Spain: From Charles V to Philip II.* (Routledge, A.D. 1997), pp. 45–46.]

[142] **The Holy League:** was a military and political coalition formed by Emperor Maximilian I of the Holy Roman Empire, Spain under Ferdinand II, and England under Henry VIII. It aimed to check the expansion of French power in Italy following France's alliance with Venice during the Italian Wars, thereby safeguarding the territorial integrity of the Papal States and their allies.

> [Mallett, Michael and Shaw, Christine. *The Italian Wars 1494–1559: War, State and Society in Early Modern Europe.* (Pearson Education, A.D. 2012), pp. 88–90.]

The Legacy of Pope Leo

In A.D. 1513, France suffered a significant defeat at the Battle of Novara, which forced the French to seek reconciliation with Rome. The schismatic cardinals who had opposed the papacy under Julius II were pardoned, and France was reintegrated into the Lateran Council that Leo had continued. However, this brief period of success soon gave way to political uncertainty. France attempted to form an alliance with Spain and sought Milan and Genoa through a matrimonial union. Leo, worried about the independence of the Papal States and the potential dominance of France in Italy, engaged in complex diplomacy, negotiating with various powers but refusing to commit to any particular side.

In A.D. 1514, Leo succeeded in brokering an Anglo-French alliance, but this shift in policy was short-lived. The pope's fear of French supremacy soon overtook his concerns about Spain, and he began negotiating in an increasingly disloyal manner with both France and its adversaries. His indecision reached a climax with the death of King Louis XII in A.D. 1515 and the ascension of the young and ambitious *Francis I.*[143] Leo, who had hoped for a favorable

---

[143] **Francis I:** was King of France from A.D. 1515 to 1547, was a dynamic and ambitious monarch whose accession marked a turning point in the Italian Wars. His desire to expand French influence in Italy and assert dominance over rival

arrangement with the late king, now found himself confronting a new and formidable monarch.

After Francis I's decisive victory at the Battle of Marignano in September, A.D. 1515, Leo X was forced to abandon his neutrality and seek reconciliation with the French king. The pope was compelled to make significant territorial concessions, surrendering Parma and Piacenza, which had been part of the Papal States and were now to be ceded to the French. In a pivotal moment of diplomacy, Leo met with King Francis at Bologna, where they reached the French Concordat of A.D. 1516. This agreement had far-reaching consequences for the Church, as it revoked the *Pragmatic Sanction of Bourges*[144] (A.D. 1438), a decree that had been hostile to papal authority.

---

powers, including the Papal States and the Holy Roman Empire, significantly intensified the political and military conflicts of the period.

    [Scarisbrick, J.J. *Francis I.* (University of California Press, A.D. 1968), pp. 3–7.]

[144] **Pragmatic Sanction of Bourges:** was an edict issued by King Charles VII of France that limited papal authority within the French Church. It asserted the superiority of general church councils over the pope, restricted papal appointments of bishops and abbots, and promoted the system of conciliarism, thereby enhancing royal control over ecclesiastical matters in France.

    [Partner, Peter. *The Lands of St. Peter: The Papal State in the Middle Ages and the Early Renaissance.* (University of California Press, A.D. 1972), pp. 261–263.]

The Legacy of Pope Leo

The revocation of the Pragmatic Sanction allowed the French king to appoint bishops, abbots, and priors, thereby granting him considerable control over the French Church. In exchange for this, Leo X secured France's formal return to the fold of the Catholic Church, ending the schismatic tendencies that had long existed in France. While this diplomatic victory secured France's allegiance to the papacy, it came at a significant cost. The French crown's increased influence over the Church led to widespread discontent among the French clergy and parliaments. The abolition of the Pragmatic Sanction alienated those who supported the conciliar system of church governance, and the abolition of free ecclesiastical elections caused lasting resentment.

The French Concordat[145] is often viewed as a short-term success for the papacy, as it ensured that France would no longer remain a schismatic force. However, the long-term consequences were less favorable. The increased royal control over the French Church would

---

[145] **The French Concordat:** was a landmark agreement between Pope Leo X and King Francis I, reached after the French victory at Marignano. It revoked the Pragmatic Sanction of Bourges and granted the French monarch the right to nominate bishops and abbots, significantly increasing royal influence over the Church in France while restoring formal papal authority and ending France's schismatic tendencies.

[Hale, J.R. *Renaissance Europe: Individual and Society 1480–1520.* (Fontana Press, A.D. 1981), pp. 278–280.]

lead to abuses of power that would cause significant problems for the Church in the years to come. Despite this, the Concordat remained in effect for centuries and served as a symbol of the delicate balance of power between the papacy and secular rulers in the early modern period.

In conclusion, Leo X's political and religious policies were marked by indecision, opportunism, and significant compromises. While he succeeded in maintaining the papacy's influence over France, his negotiations often lacked consistency, and the long-term effects of his concessions would prove detrimental to the Church. His pontificate highlights the complex relationship between papal authority and secular powers during the Renaissance and the challenges of maintaining both political stability and religious integrity in a rapidly changing Europe.

Lateran Council

Pope Leo X's pontificate was marked by his continued efforts to address the internal reforms of the Church, particularly through the Lateran Council, which had been ongoing since before his election to the papacy. As the council approached its close, it had made several significant decrees aimed at addressing the moral and administrative crises within the Church. Yet, despite the noble intentions behind these reforms, they were not fully realized, and the challenges to the Church's integrity remained unresolved.

One of the most pressing concerns for Leo X and the council was the rise of pagan Humanism and its influence on the spiritual life. Philosophers like Pietro Pompanazzi of Padua, who denied the immortality of the soul, were seen as a direct threat to the Church's doctrines. The Lateran Council responded by issuing decrees to counter these false philosophical teachings and to reinforce traditional Christian values. At the same time, a new wave of philosophical and theological studies began to emerge, seeking to defend the faith against the encroachments of Humanism.

The ninth session of the Lateran Council, held in A.D. 1516, was particularly notable for its comprehensive reforms of the Curia and the Church's administrative structure. A decree was promulgated that established guidelines for the bestowal of abbeys and benefices, ensuring that they would be granted only to individuals of merit and in accordance with canon law. Several measures were introduced to combat the widespread abuse of ecclesiastical positions. Among these reforms were restrictions on the granting of benefices, a ban on commendatory benefices, and efforts to regulate ecclesiastical depositions and transfers. These changes aimed to curb the rampant practice of simony (the selling of church offices) and the abuse of Church revenues for secular purposes. Furthermore, it was decreed that blasphemers, immoral clergy, and those engaged in negligent or simoniac practices were to be severely punished, signaling the council's intent to restore morality within the clergy.

The council also called for significant reforms in the way the Curia was administered, emphasizing the importance of a moral and virtuous lifestyle for cardinals and clergy. In an effort to ensure that the faithful were properly cared for, the council stressed the importance of religious education for children and called for a stricter approach to preaching and the cure of souls. However, despite these ambitious goals, the reforms were not rigorously enforced, and many of the Council's intentions were left unfulfilled.

The eleventh session of the Lateran Council focused on preaching and the moral state of the clergy. It was during this session that Gianfrancesco Pico della Mirandola, a highly cultured layman, delivered a poignant speech on the urgent need for a reform of morals within the Church. His speech painted a grim picture of the clergy's moral decay, lamenting the widespread corruption and abuses that plagued the Church. He warned that if the Church's moral failings were not addressed, the Church would face divine judgment, with God Himself purging the "rotten limbs" of the institution with fire and sword. This prophetic warning proved prescient, as the very same year, the conditions described by Pico della Mirandola began to manifest in the most catastrophic manner with the Protestant Revolt.

Despite the salutary decrees passed by the Lateran Council, such as the abolition of pluralism (the holding of multiple church offices by one individual), the commending of benefices, and the granting of ecclesiastical positions to children, these reforms were rarely put into practice. Leo X himself, while overseeing the council, did not hesitate to override its decrees when it suited his interests, often placing political considerations above the need for reform. The Roman Curia, which was widely despised at the time, remained just as worldly and corrupt as before. The papacy's inability or unwillingness to regulate immoral conduct among the curial courtiers and the clergy undermined the reforms' credibility and effectiveness.

Pope Leo X

The political struggles of the time further complicated matters, and Leo's focus on political alliances and the preservation of papal power often overshadowed the reforms initiated by the council. The external political challenges, including the Holy League and the pressures from various European powers, contributed to the premature conclusion of the council in A.D. 1517, long before it had the chance to fully implement the reforms that had been promised.

In the end, the Lateran Council under Leo X stands as a testament to the difficulties of internal reform within the Church during this turbulent period. While the council's decrees were commendable in their scope, they were not sufficiently enforced, and the underlying moral and administrative issues within the Church remained largely unaddressed. The council's failure to enact meaningful reform laid the groundwork for the religious upheavals that would follow in the next century, the outbreak of the Protestant Revolt beginning in A.D. 1517. The warnings of Pico della Mirandola and others would soon be realized, as the Church's failure to cleanse itself of corruption would lead to widespread dissatisfaction and the eventual splintering of Christendom.

Papal Politics, War, and Conspiracy

A.D. 1516 marked a turbulent period for Pope Leo X, who found himself navigating complex political alliances and internal Church dissent. His political decisions during this time exemplify his constant shifting allegiances and the challenges of maintaining papal authority amidst a volatile European landscape.

In March, A.D. 1516, Emperor Maximilian crossed the Alps to engage in war with the French and Venetians. As was typical of Leo's diplomatic style, he initially wavered in his support, siding with the French when their position appeared advantageous. However, his previous double-dealing had soured relations with King Francis I, who, feeling betrayed, soon adopted an antipapal policy. This turn in relations forced Leo to shift his position, and he became increasingly unfriendly toward Francis. The tension between the two was exacerbated by the issue of the Duchy of Urbino.

When the French invasion of Italy occurred, the Duke of Urbino had failed to provide the aid he was obligated to offer Leo. In retaliation, Leo exiled the Duke and awarded the Duchy to his nephew, Lorenzo de' Medici. This decision, intended to secure the Pope's interests in central Italy, deeply angered King Francis, who had ambitions for Italian territories. As a result, when Francis and Emperor Maximilian formed the League of Cambrai in A.D. 1517, which included plans to partition Upper and Central Italy, Pope Leo found himself in a precarious and isolated position. His policy of constant vacillation left him without strong allies, and his kingdom became surrounded by potentially hostile forces.

The Pope's precarious political position was made worse by the reconquest of Urbino by the exiled Duke, further undermining Leo's authority. Adding to this turmoil, a conspiracy emerged within the College of Cardinals, targeting the Pope's life. The ringleader of the plot was Cardinal Petrucci, a young and worldly ecclesiastic who was focused on money and pleasure. Petrucci, along with other cardinals who had supported Leo's election, grew discontent with the Pope's policies. Leo's refusal to comply with their excessive demands, combined with the ongoing war with Urbino, and his abolition of the election capitulations (which had given undue privileges to the cardinals), created a climate of dissatisfaction within the Vatican.

Petrucci's personal grudge against Leo was fueled by his resentment over the Pope's removal of his brother from the government of Siena. In an attempt to rid himself of the Pope,

The Legacy of Pope Leo

Petrucci conspired to poison Leo through a physician. However, the plot was foiled when suspicion was raised, and a letter revealed the scheme. An investigation ensued, implicating several other cardinals: Sauli, Riario, Soderini, and Castellesi. While their full involvement in the conspiracy could not be proven, it was clear that they had at least entertained the idea of supporting Petrucci's plan.

Petrucci was executed for his role in the conspiracy, and the other implicated cardinals were severely punished. Among them, Cardinal Riario faced a hefty fine of 150,000 ducats—an enormous sum meant to underline the seriousness of the offense. Despite the attempted assassination, Leo X remained in power, but the incident left a stain on his papacy and illustrated the dangerous combination of political intrigue and discontent within the papal court.

In summary, the period of A.D. 1516 witnessed Pope Leo X struggling with both external political threats and internal conspiracies that revealed the volatile nature of his papacy. His efforts to maintain political neutrality and balance alliances ultimately led to isolation, while the discontent among the cardinals highlighted the internal rot that undermined his authority. The assassination plot was but one example of the broader challenges Leo faced as he navigated the treacherous waters of Renaissance politics and papal governance.

Papal Corruption, War with Urbino, and the Failed Crusade Against the Turks

The aftermath of the conspiracy against Pope Leo X revealed a shocking degree of corruption and moral decay within the highest ecclesiastical circles. Despite the scandal surrounding the conspiracy, Leo displayed remarkable indifference to the consequences of his actions. Instead, he used the occasion to appoint thirty-one new cardinals, many of whom were chosen not for their merit or piety, but because of the large sums of money they provided. This move ensured that the college of cardinals became entirely submissive to his will, while also offering Leo the financial resources necessary to continue his war with Urbino.

The new appointments did not solely benefit the Pope's political interests. Some of these cardinals were virtuous and distinguished men, which, while not eradicating the corruption, did introduce some level of dignity into the Sacred College. However, the larger significance of this action was the assertion of papal authority—Leo's actions effectively cemented the superiority of the

Pope over the cardinals, asserting his control over the Church's decision-making processes.

While Leo's political maneuvering in the Vatican advanced his influence, the war with Urbino, a conflict exacerbated by Francis I of France and Emperor Maximilian, continued to drain the papal coffers. The war, which had begun with Leo's refusal to grant the Duchy of Urbino back to its rightful Duke, was finally brought to a close in A.D. 1517. The Duke of Urbino had been successfully ousted, and the Duchy remained in the hands of Lorenzo de' Medici, Leo's nephew. The war had, however, cost the papal treasury dearly, leaving it nearly empty.

With his military difficulties somewhat resolved, Leo turned his attention to the Crusade against the Turks, a cause he had supported since the early days of his papacy. Leo's zeal for a Crusade was consistent with the ancient tradition of the Holy See, but his attempts to rally European princes to this cause were largely unsuccessful. In November, A.D. 1517, he submitted an exhaustive memorial to the rulers of Europe, urging them to join forces in a unified Crusade against the Ottoman Empire. His appeal, however, was met with skepticism and reluctance from the European powers.

Pope Leo X

Each prince was more concerned with their own national interests than with the fight against the Turks, and this division severely weakened the Pope's plan.

Despite the lack of cooperation, Leo took active measures to counter the Ottoman threat. Religious processions were organized, a five-year truce was declared across Christendom, and the Crusade was publicly preached in A.D. 1518. Yet, the Pope's efforts met with little success. The international prestige of the papacy suffered a significant blow when *Cardinal Wolsey,*[146] the Lord Chancellor of England, thwarted the Pope's peaceful efforts, further diminishing Leo's ability to unite Europe for the Crusade.

When the Crusade was preached in Germany, the reaction was far from what the Pope had hoped. A large section of the German people was hostile to the Curia, believing that the papal

---

[146] **Cardinal Thomas Wolsey:** serving as England's Lord Chancellor and a cardinal under Pope Leo X, significantly impacted the papacy's international standing by orchestrating the Treaty of London in A.D. 1518. This treaty, a non-aggression pact among major European powers, was designed by Wolsey to position England as a central mediator in European affairs. While Pope Leo X had envisioned a five-year truce to unite Christendom against the advancing Ottoman Empire, Wolsey's treaty effectively sidelined the papal initiative, diminishing the Holy See's role as the arbiter of European peace. The Pope's disappointment was evident in correspondence from Cardinal Medici to Cardinal Campeggio, expressing that Wolsey's actions had deprived the Holy See of its mediating authority and strained relations between England and the papacy.
[Gwyn, Peter. *The King's Cardinal: The Rise and Fall of Thomas Wolsey.* (London: Barrie & Jenkins, A.D. 1990), p. 58.]

efforts were merely a ploy to extract more money from the faithful. The public sentiment was captured by a spiteful pamphlet, which claimed that the true Turks were not the Ottoman invaders but rather the corrupt officials of the Church itself. The pamphlet ridiculed the papacy, declaring that these "demons" in Italy could only be pacified by streams of gold.

As A.D. 1519 progressed, Leo's Crusade became increasingly entangled in political rivalries. The succession to the imperial throne of the Holy Roman Empire overshadowed the Crusade's religious significance. Maximilian I, seeking to secure the throne for his grandson Charles of Spain, found a rival in Francis I of France. Both monarchs vied for the Pope's favor, promising to take action against the Turks if Leo would support their respective claims to the imperial throne.

By the time the imperial election occurred, the Crusade had been relegated to a secondary concern. Leo's hopes of uniting Europe against the Ottoman threat were dashed, as the political maneuvering surrounding the imperial succession took precedence over religious unity. With the election of *Charles V*[147] as Holy Roman

Emperor in A.D. 1519, the prospects of a united European effort

against the Turks seemed increasingly distant.

In conclusion, Pope Leo X's papacy was marked by a

combination of corruption, political missteps, and failed crusading

efforts. While he managed to strengthen his control over the Church

by manipulating the College of Cardinals, his broader political and

religious ambitions faced insurmountable obstacles. His failure to

secure a Crusade against the Turks and the ongoing internal

corruption of the Church were indicative of the larger challenges

faced by the Renaissance papacy. Leo's reign ended in

disillusionment, as his efforts to unite Christendom for a holy cause

ultimately fell short.

---

[147] **Charles V:** was Holy Roman Emperor from A.D. 1519 to 1556. Charles
inherited an immense empire that included Spain, the Habsburg lands in Central
Europe, the Netherlands, and the Spanish Americas. His reign was marked by
constant wars against France, the Ottoman Empire, and the Protestants, as well as
a complex relationship with the papacy, particularly during the reign of Leo X and
the rise of Martin Luther. His vast dominion made him the most powerful
monarch of his age but also burdened him with impossible responsibilities and
ceaseless political entanglements.
  [Parker, Geoffrey. *Emperor: A New Life of Charles V.* (Yale University Press,
  A.D. 2019), pp. 22–24.]

Imperial Succession

Pope Leo X's attitude toward the imperial succession was primarily shaped by his anxiety regarding the power and independence of the Holy See, as well as the freedom of Italy. For Leo, the election of the Holy Roman Emperor was not just a matter of dynastic politics; it had profound implications for the balance of power in Europe, particularly for the Papacy's autonomy and its control over Italian territories. Neither of the two leading candidates, Charles of Spain or Francis I of France, was entirely acceptable to Leo, though Charles was, in the Pope's view, the lesser evil.

Leo saw the potential preponderance of power that would result from Charles's accession to the imperial throne with deep concern. The Pope feared that a strong and centralized Holy Roman Empire under Charles would undermine the freedom of Italy and diminish the political influence of the Papacy. Francis I, while also not entirely agreeable to Leo, was viewed more favorably due to his relatively weaker position compared to the might of the Spanish crown. Nonetheless, both candidates were far from ideal in the Pope's eyes.

Pope Leo X

In an attempt to protect the Papal States and maintain Italian independence, Leo's preferred outcome was the election of a German *electoral prince*,[148] someone like the Elector of Saxony or, later, the Elector of Brandenburg. These figures were seen as potential allies who might keep the Holy Roman Empire from becoming too powerful. However, Leo's position was precarious, and he was forced to play a delicate political game, "sailing with two compasses," as he sought to balance his interests by engaging with both Charles and Francis.

Leo's political maneuvering was marked by a double game, playing both rivals off against each other with matchless skill. His diplomacy was rooted in the idea of maintaining the Papal States' independence while attempting to retain friendly relations with both candidates. He even managed to conclude simultaneous alliances with both Francis I and Charles, a remarkable feat of deceit and

---

[148] **An electoral prince:** (or Kurfürst), was one of the seven high-ranking nobles of the Holy Roman Empire who held the exclusive right to elect the emperor. During Leo X's papacy, the pope favored the election of a less powerful German prince—such as Frederick the Wise, Elector of Saxony, or Joachim I Nestor, Elector of Brandenburg—hoping to prevent the empire from falling under the overwhelming influence of either the Habsburgs (Charles of Burgundy) or the French monarchy (Francis I).

[Rabe, Horst. *Reich und Reformation 1517–1555*. (Vandenhoeck & Ruprecht, A.D. 1989), pp. 40–42.]

insincerity, reflecting the Pope's willingness to do whatever necessary to protect the Papal interests. While such double-dealing might be criticized, it must be remembered that Leo's situation was fraught with challenges. He was attempting to preserve the freedom of Italy amidst growing external pressures and the ambitions of two powerful monarchs.

The death of Maximilian I in January A.D. 1519 ended Leo's diplomatic hesitation. With the Emperor's passing, the succession to the throne became urgent, and Leo's previous strategy of trying to raise up a German elector was now untenable. As the prospect of Charles becoming Emperor grew more likely, Leo shifted his focus. He began to work more fervently for Francis I, hoping to secure a firm friendship with the French king in case Charles's election became inevitable. This was a shrewd political move, as Leo knew that if Charles were elected, he would need to secure Francis's loyalty to safeguard the Papal States and Italian autonomy.

However, as the election results became clearer and Charles's victory seemed increasingly unavoidable, Leo's tactics shifted again. In the final moments, when Charles's election was almost a certainty, Leo reluctantly aligned himself with the Spanish candidate. This shift marked a political realignment, reflecting Leo's pragmatic approach to the changing dynamics of the imperial election. Although Leo's eventual support for Charles was necessary, it did not come without great anxiety. After the election, Leo watched with trepidation, uncertain about how Charles V would behave as Emperor and what his policy would be toward Italy and the Papal States.

In conclusion, Pope Leo X's political dealings during the imperial succession reflect the complexity and cynicism of Renaissance papal diplomacy. While his actions may have been viewed as deceitful, they were driven by a deep concern for the Holy See's power, the independence of Italy, and the precarious position of the Papacy in the face of rising European powers. Leo's mastery of diplomacy allowed him to navigate the delicate balance between Charles and Francis, but it was clear that his ultimate goal was to preserve the freedom and autonomy of the Papal States in an increasingly hostile and uncertain political landscape.

The Reformation

The Protestant Revolt—referred to as the "Reformation" by Protestant and modern historians—which began in A.D. 1517, stands as the most significant event of Pope Leo X's pontificate and the one with the gravest consequences for the Catholic Church. The movement, led by Martin Luther, would forever alter the course of Christian history and set in motion the fragmentation of the Church. While the religious, political, and social conditions of Germany contributed to this revolution, the immediate cause of Luther's challenge to the Church lay in the greed and corruption within the Roman Curia, which had been long brewing beneath the surface.

The events leading up to the Reformation were rooted in centuries of discontent. This discontent reached a boiling point due to Luther's criticisms, which ignited a widespread movement. The direct catalyst for Luther's actions was closely tied to the indulgence system, a practice that had become increasingly controversial and exploitative. Pope Leo X was in the process of financing the construction of St. Peter's Basilica in Rome, and to fund this monumental project, the sale of indulgences was used as a primary means of raising money. This practice not only seemed to demean the sacredness of the Church but also deeply offended the moral and theological sensibilities of many, including Luther.

Pope Leo X

One of the specific grievances that Luther targeted was the situation involving Albert of Brandenburg, who had already been granted the Archbishopric of Magdeburg. In an effort to offset his considerable debts, Albert was given the Archbishopric of Mainz and the Bishopric of Hallerstadt. However, the additional responsibility came with a taxation of 10,000 ducats, a sum that was far above the usual confirmation fees. To help him meet these demands, Rome permitted the preaching of plenary indulgences in Albert's territories, promising full forgiveness for those who contributed financially to the construction of St. Peter's Basilica. Albert was allowed to keep half of the proceeds, creating an environment rife with corruption and greed. This scandal reflected the moral decay at the heart of the Church's operations and contributed to the growing resentment towards the papacy.

Indulgences, initially intended as a means of granting forgiveness for sins, had become corrupted. While the practice was intended as an accessory to Christian life, it had evolved into a central feature of fundraising for the Church. The "Indulgences for the Dead" were particularly controversial, as they were often seen as a manipulation of the faithful's piety and fear. This deepening abuse of the indulgence system was one of the main grievances that Luther voiced, but it was also indicative of a larger problem within the Church's leadership and its approach to spiritual matters.

At a moment when the Church faced its gravest crisis in centuries, Pope Leo X failed to rise to the occasion. His response to the Reformation was marked by a lack of recognition of the gravity of the situation and a fundamental misunderstanding of the underlying causes of Luther's revolt. Rather than acknowledging the moral failings and institutional abuses that were fueling the discontent, Leo remained preoccupied with his own political concerns. His obsession with the imperial election and his entanglement in secular affairs caused him to overlook the spiritual crisis brewing within his own domain. The so-called "Reformation" did not reform the Church; it fractured Christian civilization, unleashing centuries of religious conflict and leading hundreds of millions into various heresies. Far from being merely a theological dispute, it was a sweeping social and political upheaval, cloaked in the language of reform but aimed at dismantling the spiritual and institutional unity of Christendom.

Pope Leo X

Instead of taking vigorous reformative measures, Leo chose to pursue his own pleasures and indulgences. His failure to grasp the severity of the moment and his inattention to the moral and theological upheaval created by the Reformation would prove disastrous for the Catholic Church. Leo's papacy, marked by extravagant patronage and indulgence in worldly pleasures, led him to miss the opportunity for meaningful reform. His lack of leadership in addressing the issues raised by Luther left the Church vulnerable to a deepening schism.

The "Reformation" highlighted the deep flaws within the papacy during Leo X's reign. His refusal to address the underlying causes of Luther's revolt, coupled with his focus on maintaining political alliances and his personal indulgences, led to the Church's failure to stave off the crisis that would forever change Christendom. While Leo X might have hoped to continue enjoying the wealth and influence that came with his papacy, the "Reformation" would eventually challenge the very authority of the Papal See and mark the beginning of a new era in Christian history.

Final Political Efforts and Legacy

In the final years of his pontificate, Pope Leo X directed his political energies toward expanding the States of the Church and securing its dominance in Central Italy. His ambition for territorial expansion led him to set his sights on Ferrara, aiming to consolidate power in the region. In A.D. 1519, he entered into a treaty with Francis I of France, aligning himself against Emperor Charles V, reflecting his constant political maneuvering. This alliance, however, was short-lived, as the ongoing "Lutheran Reformation" and the persistent selfishness and encroachments of the French led him to shift allegiances. True to his double-dealing nature, Leo soon pivoted and reconciled with Charles V, ultimately forming a defensive alliance with the emperor in A.D. 1521. This alliance's goal was to expel the French from Italy, a military objective that was eventually realized after some difficulty. The allies occupied Milan and Lombardy, marking a temporary political victory.

However, this military success was marred by the pope's sudden death from a malignant malaria in A.D. 1521, a tragic end to a papacy that had been marked more by indulgence than by spiritual leadership. Despite the pope's achievements in political affairs, his death was quickly followed by a simple funeral, quite unlike the grand

ceremonies often reserved for popes of his stature. It was not until

the reign of Pope Paul III (A.D. 1534-1549) that a monument was

finally erected in his honor at the Church of Santa Maria sopra

Minerva, though the monument itself was seen as cold and prosaic,

hardly fitting for a pope who was known for his extravagant

patronage of the arts.

In the wake of Leo's death, the broader assessment of his

pontificate was overwhelmingly negative, especially in regard to the

Church's well-being. Critics, such as Sigismondo Tizio, an

unflinching supporter of the Holy See, condemned Leo for his

excessive indulgence in pleasures—plays, music, and hunting—at the

expense of his responsibilities as the spiritual leader of the Church.[149]

Tizio noted that Leo's failure to seriously address the needs of his

flock and his lack of concern for their spiritual misfortunes

contributed to a disastrous papacy that failed to lead the Church

through one of its most critical moments. The "Lutheran

Reformation," which gained momentum during Leo's reign, was

---

[149] Pastor, Ludwig von. *History of the Popes from the Close of the Middle Ages. Vol. 7. Translated by Frederick Ignatius Antrobus.* (London: Kegan Paul, Trench, Trübner & Co., A.D. 1908).

largely left unaddressed and soon gave rise to a host of other heresies that spread across world splintering the unity of Christianity, while the pope remained preoccupied with political intrigues and the enticements of worldly pleasure.

Historian Von Reumont remarked that Leo X's papacy was largely to blame for the decline in faith in the integrity and moral authority of the papacy.[150] Under his leadership, the Church lost much of its moral and regenerating power, and the trust placed in the papacy by the faithful eroded. Leo's papacy was seen as a turning point when the old true spirit of the Church was extinguished in the minds of many, leaving behind a legacy of moral laxity and spiritual neglect.

In conclusion, the verdict on Leo X's papacy is clear: it was ultimately unfortunate for the Church. His lack of attention to the Church's moral and spiritual needs, his obsession with secular power, and his indulgence in personal pleasures left the papacy weakened and vulnerable at a time when it needed strong, focused leadership. His reign, though marked by grandeur and cultural achievement, was

---

[150] Reumont, Alfred von. *History of the Popes, Their Church and State, Vol. 3. Translated by Lady Mary Loyd. London.* (Longmans, Green, and Co., A.D. 1882), pp. 210–215.

ultimately one of failure in its most critical mission—the spiritual

guidance and moral leadership of the Catholic Church.

Chapter XI

Pope Leo XI (A.D. 1065)

A Brief but Principled Papacy

Born in Florence in A.D. 1535, Alessandro Ottaviano de'
Medici, later known as Pope Leo XI, was the son of Francesca
Salviati, a daughter of Giacomo Salviati, and Lucrezia Medici, the
sister of Pope Leo X. Alessandro's early years were marked by a life
of deep piety, and from a young age, he harbored a strong desire to
join the clergy. However, he struggled to gain his mother's approval
to enter the ecclesiastical state. After her death, Alessandro pursued
his religious calling. He was ordained a priest and eventually sent as
the ambassador of Grand Duke Cosimo I of Tuscany to Pope Pius
V, a position he held for an impressive fifteen years.

His career within the Church flourished under subsequent
popes. In A.D. 1573, Pope Gregory XIII appointed him Bishop of

Pistoia, followed by his promotion to Archbishop of Florence in

A.D. 1574. By A.D. 1583, he was made a Cardinal, further cementing

his position within the Church hierarchy. His diplomatic talents came

to the fore in A.D. 1596 when Pope Clement VIII appointed him as

legate to France. There, he played a pivotal role in repressing the

Huguenot[151] influence at the court of King Henry IV and worked

tirelessly to help restore the Catholic religion in France.

In A.D. 1600, Alessandro became Bishop of Albano, and by

A.D. 1602, he was transferred to the suburbicarian diocese of

Palestrina. Throughout his career, he maintained a close, spiritual

friendship with *Saint Philip Neri,*[152] whose guidance and counsel

Alessandro valued deeply. Neri, a prominent figure in the *Counter-*

---

[151] **Huguenots:** refers to French Protestants of the 16th- and 17th-centuries A.D. who adhered to the Reformed (Calvinist) tradition. They faced severe persecution in predominantly Catholic France, leading to a series of conflicts known as the French Wars of Religion. The Edict of Nantes in A.D. 1598 granted them limited rights, but its revocation in A.D. 1685 by the Edict of Fontainebleau led to renewed persecution and a significant exodus of Huguenots from France.
[Smiles, Samuel. *The Huguenots in France.* (London: John Murray, A.D. 1873), pp. 1–5.]

[152] **Saint Philip Neri:** (A.D. 1515–1595), was an Italian Catholic priest known for founding the Congregation of the Oratory, a society of secular clergy dedicated to prayer and preaching. Renowned for his personal holiness, humility, and sense of humor, Neri played a significant role in the spiritual renewal of Rome during the Counter-Reformation. His emphasis on personal piety and pastoral care made him a central figure in revitalizing the Catholic faith in the city.
[Bacci, Pietro Giacomo. *The Life of Saint Philip Neri, Apostle of Rome and Founder of the Congregation of the Oratory. Translated by F. W. Faber.* (London: Burns & Oates, A.D. 1902), pp. 45–50.]

Reformation,[153] is believed to have predicted Alessandro's future election to the papacy during their time together.

On 14 March, A.D. 1605, following the death of Pope Clement VIII, a conclave of sixty-two cardinals was convened. Among the most prominent candidates were the historian Baronius and the renowned Jesuit theologian *Robert Bellarmine.*[154] However, Aldobrandini, the leader of the Italian faction within the College of Cardinals, formed an alliance with the French party to secure the election of Alessandro. Despite opposition from King Philip III of Spain, who had his own preferred candidate, Alessandro was elected Pope Leo XI on 1 April, A.D. 1605, at the age of 70.

Leo XI's papacy, however, was brief. Shortly after his

---

[153] **The Counter-Reformation:** also known as the Catholic Reformation, was the period of Catholic revival initiated in response to the Protestant Revolt, also known as the Reformation. It began with the Council of Trent (A.D. 1545–1563), which addressed doctrinal issues and reformed clerical practices. The movement included the establishment of new religious orders, such as the Jesuits, and emphasized the importance of education, missionary work, and the reaffirmation of traditional Catholic beliefs.
  [O'Connell, Marvin R. *The Counter Reformation: 1559–1610.* (New York: Harper & Row, A.D. 1974), pp. 10–15.]
[154] **Robert Bellarmine:** (A.D. 1542–1621), was an Italian Jesuit cardinal and a leading figure in the Counter-Reformation. He served as Archbishop of Capua and was later made a cardinal. Bellarmine was renowned for his theological writings, particularly his defenses of Catholic doctrine against Protestant criticisms. His works contributed significantly to the Church's efforts to clarify and reaffirm its teachings during a time of religious upheaval.
  [Brodrick, James. *Robert Bellarmine: Saint and Scholar.* (Westminster, MD: Newman Press, A.D. 1961), pp. 120–125.]

coronation, he fell gravely ill. During his sickness, he faced intense pressure from the Curia and foreign ambassadors to grant the cardinalate to one of his grandnephews, whom he held dear and had personally educated. Despite his strong familial affection, Leo XI held a deep aversion to nepotism, a principle he refused to compromise on, even in the face of significant pressure. When his confessor encouraged him to bestow this honor upon his grandnephew, Leo XI dismissed him and sought out another confessor to prepare for his impending death. The papacy of Leo XI lasted a mere twenty-seven days, and he passed away on 27 April, A.D. 1605, less than a month after his election.

Leo XI's brief pontificate was marked by a strong commitment to moral integrity and an unwavering resistance to the corruption of nepotism, despite the immense political pressures of his time. His dedication to reform within the Church and his personal piety, which had characterized his entire life, were reflected in his final acts. His refusal to appoint his grandnephew as cardinal was a final testament to his resolve to uphold the integrity of the papal office, even as he faced the realities of illness and imminent death.

While Leo XI did not have the opportunity to effect

significant change within the Church due to the brevity of his papacy, his actions during his short reign were consistent with the virtues he had cultivated throughout his life. His commitment to spiritual principles and his moral rectitude stand as a stark contrast to the corruption and political maneuvering that characterized much of the era's papal politics.

Chapter XII

Pope Leo XII (A.D. 1823-1829)

Noble Ranks

Annibale della Genga was born on 22 August, A.D. 1760 at the Castello della Genga in the Spoleto region of Italy. His family boasted noble roots—his father's line had been ennobled by Pope Leo XI in A.D. 1605—and his mother, Maria Luisa Periberti of Fabriano, came from distinguished stock. Of the family's ten children, Annibale was the sixth—one of seven sons and three daughters. At thirteen, he began his education at the Collegio Campana in Osimo, later continuing at the Collegio Piceno in Rome, and finally at the prestigious Accademia dei Nobili Ecclesiastici, the training ground for the Holy See's diplomatic corps. Advancing quickly, he was ordained subdeacon within four years, and in A.D.

1783, though only twenty-three years old, received special dispensation to be ordained a priest.

Della Genga was tall, striking in appearance, and of affable manner—traits that, combined with his evident talents, soon brought him to the attention of Pope Pius VII. The pope appointed him *cameriere segreto*, or private chamberlain, a role typically reserved for those groomed for higher ecclesiastical office. His rhetorical gifts were publicly displayed in A.D. 1790 when he delivered the funeral oration for *Emperor Joseph II*[155] in the Sistine Chapel—an address that managed, with great diplomatic finesse, to honor the emperor without offending Austria or compromising papal dignity.

In A.D. 1792, he was made a canon of St. Peter's Basilica, and the following year he was consecrated titular Archbishop of Tyre and appointed papal nuncio to Lucerne. In A.D. 1794, he was transferred to Cologne, where he served for eleven years. His most delicate assignment came in A.D. 1795, when Pius VII sent him as

---

[155] **Emperor Joseph II:** (A.D. 1741–1790), was Holy Roman Emperor from A.D. 1765 until his death, was a proponent of enlightened absolutism. He implemented wide-ranging reforms aimed at modernizing the Habsburg domains, including religious toleration, administrative centralization, and the reduction of papal influence over the Catholic Church. His policies, while progressive, often met resistance and had mixed success.

[Beales, Derek. *Joseph II: Against the Background of Enlightenment and Revolution.* (Cambridge: Cambridge University Press, A.D. 1987).]

nuncio extraordinary to the Diet of Ratisbon to address the mounting tensions between the German Church and *Prussia*.[156] Summoned back to Rome to consult with Cardinal Consalvi, he learned that *Napoleon*[157] wished to replace him with a more pliant figure, Bishop Bernier of Orléans. Pius VII, however, held firm, and della Genga returned to his post in Munich.

In A.D. 1798, he accompanied Cardinal Caprara to Paris in an attempt to negotiate a concordat with Napoleon Bonaparte. The mission proved fruitless—the future emperor received them coolly, and no agreement was reached. Disheartened, della Genga returned to Rome and witnessed firsthand the humiliations inflicted upon the papacy by the French occupiers. Seeking peace, he withdrew to the

---

[156] **Prussia:** a prominent German kingdom from the 16th- to the 20th-century A.D., played a pivotal role in European politics and the unification of Germany. By the late-18th-century A.D., under leaders like Frederick the Great, Prussia had established itself as a military and bureaucratic powerhouse, often clashing with Austria for dominance within the Holy Roman Empire.

    [Clark, Christopher M. *Iron Kingdom: The Rise and Downfall of Prussia, 1600– 1947.* (Cambridge, MA: Belknap Press of Harvard University Press, A.D. 2006), pp. 285-290).]

[157] **Napoleon Bonaparte:** (A.D. 1769–1821), rose to prominence during the French Revolution, eventually becoming Emperor of the French. His military campaigns reshaped Europe, and his legal and administrative reforms had lasting impacts. Napoleon's interactions with the Catholic Church were complex, culminating in the Concordat of A.D. 1801, which redefined the relationship between the Church and the French state.

    [Roberts, Andrew. *Napoleon: A Life.* (New York: Viking, A.D. 2014), pp. 312-318.]

Abbey of Monticelli—granted to him *in commendam*[158] for life by Pope

Pius VI—where he lived in semi-retirement, teaching a local choir of

peasants to play the organ and sing plainchant, quietly preparing for a

future he could not yet foresee.

Recalled to Rome

Believing his active career over, Annibale della Genga

expected to spend his final years in peaceful retirement at the Abbey

of Monticelli. There, he even prepared for death, building tombs for

himself and his mother in the abbey church. But history intervened.

With Napoleon's fall in A.D. 1814 and the return of Pius VII to

Rome, della Genga was summoned once more to service, this time as

envoy extraordinary to Paris, where he was charged with delivering

papal congratulations to the restored *King Louis XVIII*.[159]

---

[158] **"in commendam"** refers to the ecclesiastical practice of granting a church benefice—such as an abbey or bishopric—to a cleric as a temporary or honorary trust, often without requiring residence or full pastoral responsibility. By the early modern period, it had become a common way for popes to reward high-ranking clergy with income and status. In della Genga's case, the Abbey of Monticelli was given to him *in commendam for life*, meaning he retained the title and revenues of the abbey without the obligations of regular monastic governance.
  [Levillain, Philippe. *The Papacy: An Encyclopedia, Vol. 1*. (New York: Routledge, A.D. 2002), p. 755.]

[159] **King Louis XVIII:** was restored to the French throne in A.D. 1814 following Napoleon's abdication and the Treaty of Fontainebleau, largely due to the efforts of the Allied powers at the Congress of Vienna, who sought to reinstate the Bourbon monarchy as a symbol of pre-revolutionary legitimacy and European stability. At the same time, Pope Pius VII, who had been imprisoned by Napoleon

Pope Leo XII

The mission, however, provoked tension. Cardinal Consalvi, the powerful Secretary of State and official representative to all the sovereigns in Paris, took offense at what he saw as a slight to his authority. Though King Louis XVIII attempted to ease the friction, Consalvi prevailed, and della Genga was soon recalled to Rome, once again retreating to Monticelli.

Two years later, his seclusion ended when Pius VII named him cardinal of Santa Maria in Trastevere and appointed him Bishop of Sinigaglia. Ongoing health issues, however, confined him to the fresher air of Spoleto, and he never formally entered his diocese, resigning it within two years. By A.D. 1820, his health had improved enough for him to be appointed Vicar of Rome, archpriest of the Liberian Basilica, and prefect of several Roman congregations.

When Pius VII died in August, A.D. 1823, the conclave convened on 2 September and deliberated for twenty-six days. Initially, the leading candidates were Cardinal Severoli, favored by the Zelanti (the conservative faction), and Cardinal Castiglioni, the choice

since A.D. 1809 and held in Savona and later Fontainebleau, was freed and triumphantly returned to Rome in May, A.D. 1814, greeted as a spiritual and moral victor over Napoleonic oppression.

[Beales, Derek. *The Restoration and the European Balance of Power*. (London: Longman, A.D. 1963), pp. 29–35.]

of the moderates and of the Catholic powers. On the morning of 21 September, Severoli's momentum had grown significantly—he had received twenty-six votes and seemed poised for election. But Cardinal Albani, representing Austrian interests, interjected with an *imperial veto,*[160] declaring Severoli unacceptable to the emperor.

The veto enraged the Zelanti, but Severoli himself proposed a solution: shift support to della Genga. Acting quickly, they rallied behind him, and on 28 September, before the opposing factions could respond, he was triumphantly elected pope with thirty-four votes.

At first, the ailing cardinal resisted. Tearfully, he told the conclave, "You are electing a dead man." But the cardinals insisted, appealing to his sense of duty. Moved, he relented. With grace, he turned to Cardinal Castiglioni and assured him that his time would

---

[160] **Imperial veto:** or *jus exclusivae*, was a privilege claimed by certain Catholic monarchs—most notably the Holy Roman Emperor (later the Emperor of Austria), the King of France, and the King of Spain—to reject a papal candidate during a conclave. Though never formally recognized by the Church, this practice was tolerated in papal elections from the 17th-century A.D. until it was officially abolished by Pope Pius X in A.D. 1904. In the conclave of A.D. 1823, Emperor Francis I of Austria exercised this veto through Cardinal Giuseppe Albani to block Cardinal Severoli, citing political concerns. This maneuver shifted the conclave's momentum and paved the way for della Genga's election as Pope Leo XII.
[Pirie, Valérie. *The Triple Crown: An Account of the Papal Conclaves.* (London: Gollancz, A.D. 1935), pp. 263–265.]

come—he would one day be Pius VIII. Then, he announced his own papal name: Leo XII.

Church Reformer

Immediately after his election, Leo XII signaled the tone of his pontificate by appointing the elderly Cardinal della Somaglia, then in his eighties, as Secretary of State. The choice was telling—favoring continuity, conservatism, and age-old loyalties over innovation. Leo was crowned on 5 October, 1823, and his early measures made clear his intention to restore order and tradition.

He launched efforts to curb the rampant brigandage and lawlessness plaguing the provinces of Maritima and the Campagna, though with limited success. More controversially, he issued an ordinance forcing the Jews—who had moved freely into the city during the Revolutionary period—back into the confines of the *Roman Ghetto*.[161] Such measures typified Leo XII's papal outlook:

---

[161] **The Roman Ghetto:** originally established in A.D. 1555 by Pope Paul IV, had been dismantled during the French Revolutionary occupation of Rome in A.D. 1798, which granted Jews civil liberties and the right to live outside the Ghetto walls. However, with the restoration of papal authority, restrictive policies were gradually reinstated. In A.D. 1825, Pope Leo XII issued an ordinance compelling Jews to return to the Ghetto, reversing the freedoms gained during the Revolutionary and Napoleonic eras. This action was part of Leo XII's broader efforts to reassert conservative, Counter-Reformation-era policies and reimpose clerical control over social life in the Papal States.

rigorous in morals, nostalgic for the past, and determined to restore the old religious and social order.

There is something poignant in the tension between Leo's commanding intellect as head of the universal Church and his heavy-handed, often ineffective governance of the Papal States. Confronted with the tide of modernity, he positioned himself as a defender of traditional customs and institutions, lacking sympathy or understanding for the rising aspirations toward liberty sweeping across Europe.

Nonetheless, within the Church itself, he acted with vigor. He launched a stern campaign to purify the Roman Curia, targeting the corruption and incompetence that had long plagued its ranks. He actively opposed religious indifferentism and the growing influence of Protestant missionaries. *The Holy Year of 1825,*[162] proclaimed over the objections of cautious and conservative voices in the hierarchy

---

[Stow, Kenneth. *The Jews in Rome: Vol. 2, 1551–1557.* (Leiden: Brill, A.D. 1995), pp. 10–12]

[162] **The Holy Year of 1825:** was the first Jubilee celebrated after the Napoleonic wars and was intended by Pope Leo XII as a reaffirmation of Catholic faith and identity amidst the rising tides of religious indifferentism and Protestant missionary activity. Despite concerns from certain conservative clerics and Catholic monarchs, the Jubilee drew tens of thousands of pilgrims to Rome and served as a significant public demonstration of papal authority and devotion in the post-revolutionary era.

[O'Malley, John W. *A History of the Popes: From Peter to the Present.* (Lanham, MD: Sheed & Ward, A.D. 2010), pp. 271–272.]

and among Catholic rulers, proved a powerful expression of Catholic devotion.

Abroad, Leo XII defended embattled Catholics in the Netherlands and offered strategic support to the growing movement for Catholic emancipation in the British Isles, seeing it through until its final success. At home, however, public dissatisfaction with his rigid administration and reactionary policies grew steadily, and dissent was suppressed with severity by Cardinal Rivarola, his chief enforcer.

The Final Years

Leo XII's later years were marked by a deepening commitment to religious renewal, even as the complex political climate of Europe revealed the limits of his understanding and flexibility. In both France and Spain, he supported the *legitimist cause,*[163] despite the fact that it often exploited religion as a tool of political reaction. Even when these same forces—in events like the

---

[163] **Legitimist cause:** favoring the restoration and defense of traditional monarchies such as the Bourbons in France and Spain—was consistent with his broader political vision of throne-and-altar unity. This alignment often led to papal support for reactionary regimes that invoked Catholicism as a means of restoring pre-revolutionary order, even when such regimes enacted policies that conflicted with papal or ecclesiastical interests.

[Chadwick, Owen. *A History of the Popes, 1830–1914.* (Oxford: Oxford University Press, A.D. 1998), pp. 4–5.]

suppression of Jesuit schools in France or the obstruction of
episcopal appointments in Mexico—proved indifferent or hostile to
the broader interests of the Church, Leo remained aligned with them.
His loyalty to the monarchist ideal sometimes took precedence over
practical support for the Faith's flourishing.

Pope Leo continued to value the counsel of Cardinal
Consalvi, whose moderation and diplomacy had long steadied the
Vatican's course. In both Consalvi's case and that of the treasurer
Cristaldi, Leo showed magnanimity, refusing to let personal slights
cloud his recognition of talent. But Consalvi's death in A.D. 1824
deprived the Holy See of one of its wisest voices.

That same year, Leo restored the Collegio Romano to the
direction of the Jesuits, a move reflecting his zeal for revitalizing
Catholic education. In A.D. 1825, he condemned *Freemasonry*[164] and

---

[164] Pope Leo XII's condemnation of **Freemasonry** in A.D. 1825 reflected
longstanding papal hostility toward secret societies perceived as subversive to
Church and throne. Freemasonic lodges—structured as exclusive, hierarchical
fraternities with esoteric rites and oaths—served as incubators for Enlightenment
ideals and liberal revolutionary agitation. These lodges often operated
transnationally and played a significant role in promoting movements that espoused
slogans such as "Liberty, Equality, Fraternity" and the "Rights of Man." In many
parts of Europe and Latin America, Masonic networks were instrumental in
organizing revolutions, undermining traditional monarchies, and challenging the
moral and doctrinal authority of the Church.

[Ridley, Jasper. *The Freemasons: A History of the World's Most Powerful Secret
Society.* (New York: Arcade Publishing, A.D. 1999), pp. 125–145.]

other secret societies, underscoring his distrust of revolutionary undercurrents. Under his leadership, the Vatican Library was enriched, the Vatican press revived, and distinguished scholars such as Zurla, Martucci, and Champollion received papal encouragement. He also oversaw substantial progress in the rebuilding of the Basilica of St. Paul and worked to restore reverence and dignity in public worship.

But Leo's health, always fragile, could not keep pace with his devout energy. He nearly died in December, A.D. 1823, recovering only—according to popular belief—through the intercessory sacrifice of Bishop Vincenzo Strambi, who offered his own life in exchange for the pope's and died shortly thereafter. In early February, A.D. 1829, following a private audience with his Secretary of State, Cardinal Bernetti, Leo fell gravely ill. He received the Viaticum and anointing on 8 February, lost consciousness on the 9th, and died quietly the next morning.

Leo XII was a man of noble character and passionate conviction. He championed order, piety, and efficiency, yet he lacked the insight and sympathy required to grasp the deeper transformations of his time. His reign, though spiritually fervent, was politically rigid, leaving his successors with a diminished ability to confront the rising tide of modern challenges.

Chapter XIII

Pope Leo XIII (A.D. 1878-1903)

Early Formation

Gioacchino Vincenzo Raffaele Luigi Pecci, who would one day become Pope Leo XIII, was born on 2 March, A.D. 1810 in Carpineto, the sixth of seven sons born to Count Lodovico Pecci and Anna Prosperi-Buzi. Although the Pecci family held a noble title, their lineage was questioned in certain circles. When the young Gioacchino applied for admission to the prestigious Accademia dei Nobili in Rome, some objected on grounds of doubtful aristocratic standing. In response, he composed a detailed family history demonstrating that the Pecci of Carpineto were a cadet branch of the Pecci of Siena, who had migrated to the Papal States in the 16th-century A.D. under Pope Clement VII, having supported the Medici during a turbulent period in Florentine politics.

At the age of eight, Gioacchino and his ten-year-old brother Giuseppe were enrolled at the new Jesuit school in Viterbo—now the diocesan seminary. There, from A.D. 1818 to 1824, Gioacchino laid the foundation for the classical mastery of Latin and Italian that would later distinguish his encyclicals, papal addresses, and poetry. Much of the credit belongs to his mentor, Padre Leonardo Garibaldi, who recognized and nurtured his gifts.

When the Jesuits regained control of the Collegio Romano in A.D. 1824, the Pecci brothers transferred there to continue their studies in humanities and rhetoric. Gioacchino soon distinguished himself. At the end of his rhetoric course, he was selected to deliver the final Latin oration, choosing as his theme "The Contrast between Pagan and Christian Rome"—a subject that reflected both his intellectual range and his deepening sense of Christian civilization's mission. His three-year study of philosophy and natural sciences was equally distinguished, laying the groundwork for the synthesis of faith and reason that would define his papacy.

A Vocation Awakened and a Statesman Formed

Though his pious mother had long desired that he enter the

ecclesiastical state, Gioacchino Pecci remained for some time undecided about his vocation. Like many ambitious young Romans of the era seeking careers in public service, he pursued parallel studies in theology, canon law, and civil law. At Rome, his instructors included the eminent theologian Giovanni Perrone and the renowned scriptural scholar Patrizi—figures who deeply shaped the intellectual and doctrinal world of 19th-century A.D. Catholicism. In A.D. 1832, he received the doctorate in theology and, overcoming earlier challenges regarding his background, gained entry to the prestigious Academy of Noble Ecclesiastics. He then continued his legal studies at the Sapienza University.

Pecci's remarkable abilities, coupled with the patronage of Cardinals Sala and Pacca, soon earned him rapid advancement. In January, A.D. 1837, while still in minor orders, he was named a domestic prelate by *Pope Gregory XVI.*[165] By March, he had been

---

[165] **Pope Gregory XVI:** (reigned A.D. 1831–1846), born Bartolomeo Alberto Cappellari, was a staunch conservative who opposed modern liberalism, nationalism, and industrialization. A former Camaldolese monk and theologian, he rose to prominence as Prefect of the Propaganda Fide before his election. His A.D. 1832 encyclical *Mirari Vos* condemned religious indifferentism, freedom of the press, and separation of Church and state. Domestically, he relied on Austrian military support and an expanding secret police to quell revolts in the Papal States. Though personally austere and pious, his governance was often marked by repression and resistance to reform, earning him criticism from both liberal Catholics and secular nationalists.

appointed *Referendario della Segnatura*, a judicial office he later exchanged for a post in the *Congregazione del Buon Governo*—effectively the Ministry of the Interior of the Papal States—then under the prefecture of his patron, Cardinal Sala. During the cholera epidemic that ravaged Rome that year, Pecci distinguished himself through tireless service, coordinating the city's hospitals and emergency responses alongside the cardinal. His energy, prudence, and administrative talent persuaded Sala that Pecci's true calling lay in the priesthood, a conviction he pressed upon the young cleric with increasing urgency, even hinting that his future advancement depended on it.

Moved by this counsel and sensing the weight of responsibility ahead, Pecci received ordination on 31 December, A.D. 1837 from Cardinal Odescalchi, Vicar of Rome, in the chapel of St. Stanislaus on the Quirinal Hill. Barely a month later, he was appointed Delegate (civil governor) of Benevento, an unruly enclave of the Papal States embedded deep within the Kingdom of Naples. Long plagued by brigandage and lawlessness—vestiges of the

[Coppa, Frank J. *Pope Gregory XVI, 1831–1846: A Study in Church and State.* (Twayne Publishers, A.D. 1979), pp. 12–16, 85–92.]

173

Napoleonic wars and the counter-revolutionary *Sanfedisti*[166]—

Benevento presented a formidable challenge. Pope Gregory XVI,

seeking vigorous reform, turned to the young and energetic Mgr.

Pecci, whose name was recommended by both Cardinal Sala and

Cardinal Lambruschini, the Secretary of State.

Arriving in Benevento on 2 February, A.D. 1838, Pecci

quickly fell ill with typhoid fever, but upon his recovery launched a

relentless campaign to restore order. He cracked down not only on

the bandits but also on the local nobility who sheltered them,

wielding authority with a firmness that earned both fear and

admiration. Working closely with Mgr. di Pietro, the papal nuncio in

Naples, he established coordinated efforts with Neapolitan police,

forming an unprecedented alliance to suppress criminal networks.

His reformist zeal extended beyond security: he rebuilt roads,

---

[166] **The Sanfedisti:** members of the "Army of Holy Faith in Our Lord Jesus
Christ" (Armata della Santa Fede in nostro Signore Gesù Cristo)—were a counter-
revolutionary force mobilized in A.D. 1799 by Cardinal Fabrizio Ruffo in southern
Italy. Comprising peasants, clergy, former soldiers, and brigands, these irregular
militias aimed to restore the Bourbon monarchy and suppress the pro-French
Parthenopaean Republic. Their operations, characterized by guerrilla tactics and
religious fervor, left a legacy of lawlessness and instability in regions like
Benevento. The enduring impact of the Sanfedisti contributed to the challenges
faced by papal authorities in reasserting control and order in the post-Napoleonic
period.
[Davis, John A. *Naples and Napoleon: Southern Italy and the European
Revolutions, 1780–1860.* (Oxford University Press, A.D. 2006), pp. 260–
261.]

restructured the province's antiquated tax system—still burdened by extortionate French-imposed levies—and championed fairness in governance.

When he learned of negotiations between the Holy See and Naples to exchange Benevento for a neighboring stretch of Neapolitan territory, Pecci reacted with passion. Believing such a trade would betray both the people and the Papacy's interests, he drafted a powerful memorial to Rome. His arguments carried the day: the negotiations were promptly abandoned. In this, as in much else, Mgr. Pecci had already begun to show the resolve, diplomatic foresight, and administrative genius that would define his later papacy.

The Path to the Episcopate

The profound success Mgr. Pecci achieved during his three-year tenure as Delegate of Benevento did not go unnoticed. Recognizing in him a rare combination of firmness and prudence, Pope Gregory XVI entrusted him with another critical civil post—one requiring a no less commanding presence, albeit in a radically different context. Though initially considered for Spoleto, he was instead assigned on 17 July, A.D. 1841 to Perugia, a city seething with revolutionary fervor and a stronghold of anti-papal sentiment. Undaunted by the volatile political climate, Pecci set to work with characteristic resolve. He brought order and efficiency to the administration of justice, making it both swifter and more economical, and launched social reforms aimed at the well-being of the citizenry. Among these was the foundation of a savings bank, designed to provide small farmers and tradesmen access to credit at humane interest rates—an early testament to his social concern. He also initiated educational reforms and undertook numerous efforts to improve public life, earning both the respect and the gratitude of the population.

In January, A.D. 1843, Pecci's trajectory shifted from governance to diplomacy. He was appointed Apostolic Nuncio to Brussels, succeeding Mgr. Fornari, who had been transferred to Paris. On 19 February, he was consecrated titular Archbishop of Damiata by Cardinal Lambruschini, and shortly thereafter departed for Belgium. There, he encountered a nation divided by fierce political and religious debate, particularly surrounding the so-called "school question"—the struggle between the Catholic majority and the

Liberal minority over the control of education. Navigating this sensitive terrain with diplomatic finesse, Pecci lent decisive support to the Catholic cause, encouraging both bishops and lay leaders in defense of parochial schools, while at the same time cultivating the trust of the royal court. His tact and personal charm won over not only the devout Queen Louise, but also King Leopold I, whose Liberal leanings had previously inclined him toward suspicion of clerical influence.

Pecci's efforts in Belgium bore lasting fruit. He succeeded in unifying the fragmented Catholic factions and was the driving force behind the founding of the Belgian College in Rome in A.D. 1844, a seminal institution for the formation of Belgian clergy. In A.D. 1845, he undertook a pastoral journey through *Rhenish Prussia*[167]—visiting Cologne, Mainz, and Trier—at a time of rising tension provoked by the schismatic agitation of Johannes Ronge, a defrocked priest who

---

[167] **Rhenish Prussia:** established after the Congress of Vienna in A.D. 1815, encompassed the Catholic-dominated western provinces of the Kingdom of Prussia. These territories, formerly part of various ecclesiastical and secular principalities, became a point of tension between the Protestant Prussian monarchy and the Catholic Church, particularly as Prussia attempted to impose administrative centralization and religious conformity in the decades following the Napoleonic era.

[Sperber, Jonathan. *Rhineland Radicals: The Democratic Movement and the Revolution of 1848–1849.* (Princeton, NJ: Princeton University Press, A.D. 1991), pp. 18–21.]

had stirred controversy during the exposition of the Holy Coat of Trier in A.D. 1844. Thanks to Pecci's vigilance and influence, these disruptive forces failed to take root in Belgium.

Meanwhile, the See of Perugia had fallen vacant. Responding both to the fervent wishes of the Perugian faithful and the critical needs of that embattled region, Pope Gregory XVI recalled Mgr. Pecci from Brussels and named him Bishop of Perugia. In recognition of his diplomatic and ecclesiastical stature, he was permitted to retain the personal title of Archbishop—a fitting mark of distinction for one whose talents had already extended across the spheres of government, diplomacy, and pastoral care.

The Perugian Episcopate

With an affectionate and laudatory letter from King Leopold of Belgium in hand, Mgr. Pecci departed Brussels, pausing first in London and then in Paris, where he spent a month in each capital. These sojourns not only brought him into contact with the highest circles of European courts, but also afforded him the opportunity to engage with numerous men of distinction, among them Nicholas Wiseman, the future Cardinal and leader of the English Catholic revival. Enriched by these encounters and deeply broadened in perspective, Pecci returned to Rome on 26 May, A.D. 1846—only to find Pope Gregory XVI on his deathbed. Thus deprived of the opportunity to render an account of his diplomatic labors, he prepared to assume a new chapter in his ecclesiastical career.

On 27 July, A.D. 1846, Mgr. Pecci made his solemn entry into Perugia, the city and diocese that would remain the field of his pastoral care for the next thirty-two years. Gregory XVI had harbored the intention of raising him to the College of Cardinals, but the pope's death, along with the tumultuous early years of Pope Pius IX's pontificate, delayed the fulfillment of this design until 19 December, A.D. 1853. Though Pius IX repeatedly expressed the desire to draw him closer by offering him a suburbicarian see, Pecci steadfastly chose to remain in Perugia—perhaps in part due to his cool relationship with the powerful Cardinal Antonelli. Yet the oft-repeated claim that Pius IX kept Pecci in Perugia out of suspicion regarding his supposed liberal tendencies is without foundation; far from being a courtier of innovation, Pecci was a bishop devoted above all to the defense and diffusion of Catholic truth.

As Bishop of Perugia, his episcopate was distinguished by a

pastoral zeal both deep and methodical. He labored to instill in his flock a vibrant piety grounded in sound catechesis. He mandated that his priests preach regularly and undertake catechetical instruction not only for children but also for adults—a practice he required to be observed for at least an hour each Sunday and holy day afternoon, thus anticipating by decades the universal norms later codified by Pope Pius X in A.D. 1905. He revised and republished the diocesan catechism in A.D. 1856, and in A.D. 1857 he authored a practical manual for priests, guiding them in their sacred ministry. He frequently arranged for retreats and missions to sustain the spiritual vitality of both clergy and laity.

The aftermath of the Piedmontese occupation brought grievous challenges. The suppression of religious orders and the resulting depopulation of clerical ranks left his diocese in want of priests. To remedy this crisis, he founded in A.D. 1875 an association of diocesan missionaries, ready to serve wherever need arose. Ever attentive to the formation of a learned and virtuous clergy, he lavished extraordinary care upon his seminary, which he affectionately termed "the apple of his eye." Between A.D. 1846 and 1850, he personally financed the expansion of the seminary's buildings, enlisted outstanding professors, oversaw examinations, and at times instructed the seminarians himself. He championed the study of St. Thomas Aquinas, both in philosophy and theology, and in A.D. 1872 founded the "Accademia di San Tommaso," a project he had first conceived in A.D. 1858. In this, as in all things, Pecci showed himself a man of vision and fidelity—equally committed to the intellectual patrimony of the Church and the spiritual needs of his people.

A Champion of Education, Charity, and the Church's Temporal Power

In A.D. 1872, Mgr. Pecci made a significant contribution to the educational landscape of his diocese by introducing government-mandated standards for secondary schools and colleges. This move was part of his broader effort to standardize and improve education in the region, reflecting his commitment to both the intellectual and moral formation of youth. However, the financial stability of his beloved seminary was soon undermined when its funds were converted into state bonds, which led to a marked decrease in revenue. This setback required further personal sacrifices on the bishop's part, though he continued with unwavering resolve to fulfill his pastoral duties.

With the exception of a handful of troublesome priests, who sought refuge under the protection of the newly-established government, the discipline of the clergy in his diocese remained exemplary. To aid many of the priests who had been impoverished by the confiscation of church funds, he established in A.D. 1873 the *Society of St. Gioacchino,*[168] which provided much-needed assistance. In addition, he founded conferences of *St. Vincent de Paul*[169] to promote charitable works within the community, furthering the Church's mission to care for the poor and suffering.

Pecci's contributions to education were not confined to the academic realm alone. He reorganized and expanded many educational institutions for the youth, establishing new ones when

---

[168] **The Society of St. Gioacchino:** founded in Naples in the early-19th-century A.D., was a lay Catholic confraternity devoted to charitable works, especially aiding the poor and sick. Though not widely known outside southern Italy, it exemplified the revival of Catholic lay piety under papal encouragement in response to revolutionary and secularizing trends in Europe.
 [Davis, John A. *Conflict and Control: Law and Order in Nineteenth-Century Italy.* (New York: St. Martin's Press, A.D. 1988), p. 115.]
[169] **The Society of St. Vincent de Paul:** was founded in A.D. 1833 by Blessed Frédéric Ozanam in Paris, quickly spread throughout Europe and beyond. It organized local lay conferences committed to person-to-person charity, rooted in Catholic social teaching. These conferences became a vital tool for restoring the Church's role in poor relief, especially in post-revolutionary and post-unification contexts
 [Sickinger, Raymond L. *The Sociology of Frédéric Ozanam and the Society of St. Vincent de Paul.* (Marquette University Press, A.D. 2017), pp. 85–101.]

needed. To ensure their success, he invited religious orders from Belgium, including the Sisters of the Sacred Heart and the Brothers of Mercy, to assist in the care and instruction of the students. His dedication to the spiritual and intellectual welfare of the youth bore fruit in many forms, including the construction of thirty-six new churches within his diocese during his long tenure as bishop.

Perhaps no moment more clearly demonstrated his pastoral charity and foresight than the famine of A.D. 1854, which was precipitated by an earthquake that devastated large parts of Umbria. During this crisis, Pecci's leadership was nothing short of miraculous; through his tireless efforts, he ensured that aid reached those most in need, alleviating the suffering of countless families.

Throughout the turbulent political climate of his time, Pecci remained a staunch defender of the Holy See's temporal power. Yet, while unyielding in his support for the Church's sovereignty, he was cautious in his actions, careful to avoid provoking the new government into further hostilities. His diplomatic acumen and steady resolve helped protect the interests of the Church during one of its most challenging periods.

Pecci's Leadership

Soon after his arrival in Perugia, Mgr. Pecci found himself confronted with a popular commotion. Demonstrating his characteristic leadership and diplomatic skill, he personally intervened to calm the unrest, restoring peace to the troubled city. His talents as a mediator were called upon again in A.D. 1849, when Garibaldian bands, expelled from Rome, took refuge in the Umbrian hills. The Austrians, under Prince Liechtenstein, moved to occupy Perugia, but Pecci, recognizing the potential for heightened tension and resentment among the locals, took swift action. He journeyed to the Austrian camp and succeeded in preventing the foreign occupation, thus sparing the town from unnecessary conflict.

In A.D. 1859, as Perugia faced yet another political upheaval, a small group of outlaws established a provisional government. When they prepared to resist the advancing Pontifical troops, led by Colonel Schmidt, Pecci intervened once more, writing a heartfelt letter urging them to abandon their reckless course and avoid a senseless loss of life. Regrettably, the rebels rejected his counsel, and the result was the tragic "Massacre of Perugia" on June 20, A.D. 1859, a dark chapter in the city's history.

The Legacy of Pope Leo

As the political landscape of the region continued to shift, Pecci remained a resolute defender of the Church's temporal power. In February, A.D. 1860, he wrote a pastoral letter advocating for the necessity of the Holy See's sovereignty, standing firm in his beliefs even as political tides turned against the Papal States. That year, on September 14, Perugia and the entire region of Umbria were annexed to Piedmont, marking a profound shift in the region's governance.

Pecci's opposition to this annexation led him to repeatedly voice his objections, writing no less than eighteen protests against the various laws and decrees imposed by the new government. These included measures such as civil marriage, the suppression of religious orders and their harsh treatment, and the forced military service of clergy. Despite his vocal resistance to these policies, Pecci's tact and prudence ensured that he avoided significant confrontation with the civil authorities, and he was never subjected to any serious legal consequences. On the rare occasion he was brought before the courts, he was acquitted, further cementing his reputation for judiciousness in the face of adversity.

Rise to the Papacy

In August, A.D. 1877, following the death of Cardinal de Angelis, Pius IX appointed Mgr. Pecci as camerlengo, a position that necessitated his residence in Rome. This marked a pivotal moment in Pecci's life, setting him on a path that would soon culminate in his elevation to the papacy. When Pope Pius IX passed away on February 7, A.D. 1878, the conclave that followed was overshadowed by political intrigue. The Liberal press had persistently insinuated that the Italian Government might intervene in the conclave and occupy the Vatican, a notion that cast a shadow over the process. Yet, fate intervened—the Russo-Turkish War and the unexpected death of King Victor Emmanuel II on January 9, A.D. 1878, diverted the Government's attention. The conclave proceeded unimpeded, and after three scrutinies, Cardinal Pecci emerged victorious, securing forty-four votes out of sixty-one, a testament to his broad support among the electors.

Before his election, Pecci had penned a stirring pastoral letter to his flock, addressing the crucial relationship between the Church and civilization. The ecclesiastical world, at the time, was in a state of considerable flux. While Pius IX had earned profound respect and affection for the papacy across Christendom—even from its adversaries—the Church's relationship with civil authorities had become strained and, in many cases, distant. Despite these challenges, the diplomatic finesse of the newly elected Pope Leo XIII—Pecci's papal name—soon became evident. Through his skillful diplomacy, he was able to navigate the delicate landscape, preventing ruptures, alleviating tensions, and cultivating cordial relations with nearly all of the major powers of the time.

Papal Diplomacy and Challenges in Europe

Throughout his pontificate, Pope Leo XIII managed to maintain amicable relations with France, even committing himself to the French Government by promising to call on all Catholics to accept the Republic. Despite his efforts, however, very few monarchists heeded his call, and by the end of his life, he witnessed the eventual failure of his French policy, though he was spared the agony of witnessing the final catastrophe that, in all likelihood, even his diplomatic skill could not have prevented.

Pope Leo XIII played a pivotal role in shaping France's

alliance with Russia, offsetting the influence of *the Triple Alliance*[170]

and hoping to avoid potential conflicts, all the while expecting to gain

France's support in resolving the Roman question. However, his

diplomatic efforts with Germany were more fruitful. On the very day

of his election, Leo wrote to *Emperor Wilhelm,*[171] expressing a desire to

restore relations with the German Government. While the emperor's

response was civil yet distant, it marked the beginning of a thaw in

diplomatic relations. Soon, *Chancellor Otto von Bismarck,*[172] realizing his

inability to govern effectively with the Liberals—whom he had

---

[170] **The Triple Alliance:** concluded in A.D. 1882 between Germany, Austria-Hungary, and Italy, aimed to counterbalance French and Russian influence in Europe. It shaped the diplomatic framework of late-19th-century A.D. continental politics and complicated papal attempts to resolve the Roman Question diplomatically.
> [Langer, William L. *European Alliances and Alignments, 1871–1890.* (New York: Knopf, A.D. 1950), pp. 128–135.]

[171] **Emperor Wilhelm I:** though monarch of the newly unified German Empire, often deferred foreign and domestic policy decisions to his powerful chancellor, Otto von Bismarck. His correspondence with Pope Leo XIII in the early A.D. 1880s reflected cautious diplomacy amid the Church's attempts to reassert influence in post-Kulturkampf Germany.
> [Röhl, John C.G. *Germany Without Bismarck: The Crisis of Government in the Second Reich, 1890–1900.* (Berkeley: University of California Press, A.D. 1967), p. 37.]

[172] **Chancellor Otto von Bismarck:** architect of German unification, initially viewed the Catholic Church as a political threat and sought to marginalize it through state policy. However, following growing resistance and political necessity, he realigned his strategy, ultimately seeking cooperation with the Catholic Centre Party by the early A.D. 1880s.
> [Craig, Gordon A. *Germany: 1866–1945.* (Oxford: Oxford University Press, A.D. 1978), pp. 85–87.] 188

antagonized through the *Kulturkampf*[173]—recognized the necessity of aligning with the Catholic Centre Party.

Negotiations began as early as A.D. 1878, with Bismarck seeking a diplomatic resolution with the Vatican. By A.D. 1884, formal diplomatic relations had been re-established, and in A.D. 1887 a *modus vivendi*[174] was reached between Church and State. Bismarck, hoping for the pope's support on certain political issues, proposed that Pope Leo arbitrate disputes between Germany and Spain. This relationship was further solidified through multiple visits from *Kaiser Wilhelm II*[175] to the Vatican, demonstrating the growing bond between

---

[173] **Kulturkampf:** ("culture struggle"), was a state-led campaign in the German Empire from A.D. 1871 to 1878 that aimed to curtail the influence of the Catholic Church, particularly in education and clerical appointments. The measures, driven by Bismarck and the Prussian Liberals, led to the imprisonment and exile of clergy and the suppression of Catholic institutions until their gradual repeal.

    [Ross, Ronald J. *The Failure of Bismarck's Kulturkampf: Catholicism and State Power in Imperial Germany.* (Washington, D.C.: Catholic University of America Press, A.D. 1998), pp. 22–45.]

[174] **"modus vivendi"** was a practical arrangement to allow coexistence without resolving underlying ideological differences—reached in A.D. 1887 between the Holy See and the German Empire, easing tensions from the Kulturkampf and restoring limited Church autonomy in appointments and education.

    [Anderson, Margaret Lavinia. *Windthorst: A Political Biography.* (Oxford: Oxford University Press, A.D. 1981), pp. 364–367.]

[175] **Kaiser Wilhelm II:** who succeeded his father in A.D. 1888, sought warmer relations with the Vatican as part of a broader strategy to consolidate support from conservative and Catholic constituencies. His multiple visits to Pope Leo XIII symbolized a shift from confrontation to cooperation between the German Empire and the Catholic Church.

    [Cecil, Lamar. *Wilhelm II: Emperor and Exile, 1900–1941, Vol. 1.* (Chapel Hill: University of North Carolina Press, A.D. 1996), pp. 45–47.]

the Church and Germany.

Pope Leo also navigated tensions with Belgium, particularly over the school question, which led to a break in relations in A.D. 1880. The situation was resolved by A.D. 1883 when a new Catholic Government restored diplomatic ties. In Switzerland, the Church's position improved during Leo's pontificate, particularly in the regions of Ficino, Aargau, and Basle.

In Russia, Leo XIII sought to improve relations, especially following the A.D. 1879 assassination attempt on Tsar Alexander II and the czar's A.D. 1888 silver jubilee. While early efforts were met with resistance, particularly in the case of the Ruthenian Catholics, by A.D. 1894—after the ascension of Alexander III—diplomatic relations were once again restored. Throughout these years, Leo XIII maintained a delicate balance, carefully urging loyalty from Polish Catholics under Russian rule while navigating the complexities of international diplomacy.

Papal Influence on the English-Speaking World

Pope Leo XIII made several significant contributions that had a profound impact on the English-speaking world. Notably, he elevated *John Henry Newman*[176] to the cardinalate in A.D. 1879, an act that resonated deeply in England. In A.D. 1881, he issued the *Romanos Pontifices*, a document addressing the relations between the Catholic hierarchy and the regular clergy, and in A.D. 1886, he beatified fifty English martyrs. He also marked the thirteenth centenary of St. Gregory the Great, the Apostle of England, with a special celebration in A.D. 1891.

Pope Leo's influence extended to the realm of Catholic unity, as demonstrated in his A.D. 1895 Encyclical *Ad Anglos*, which called for the return to Catholic unity, and the A.D. 1896 *Apostolicæ Curæ*, which addressed the non-validity of Anglican orders. His actions also extended to Scotland, where in A.D. 1878 he restored the Scottish hierarchy, and in A.D. 1898, he sent a heartfelt letter to the Scottish people.

In English India, Pope Leo established the Catholic hierarchy in A.D. 1886 and worked to resolve longstanding conflicts with the

---

[176] **John Henry Newman:** (A.D. 1801–1890), was a leading figure in the Oxford Movement within the Church of England before his conversion to Roman Catholicism in A.D. 1845. A theologian, philosopher, and prolific writer, Newman emphasized the development of doctrine and the primacy of conscience. His works, such as *An Essay on the Development of Christian Doctrine* and *The Idea of a University*, remain influential in both Catholic and broader Christian thought.
    [Ker, Ian. *John Henry Newman: A Biography.* (Oxford: Oxford University Press, A.D. 1988), pp. 211–230, 370–392.]

Portuguese authorities. His engagement with Ireland was equally

notable, as he took a pastoral interest in the Irish Church on

numerous occasions. This was evident in his A.D. 1881 letter to

Archbishop McCabe of Dublin, the elevation of McCabe to the

cardinalate in A.D. 1882, and his invitation to Irish bishops to come

to Rome in A.D. 1885. Additionally, the decree of the Holy Office on

13 April, A.D. 1888 concerning the plan of campaign and boycotting,

along with the Encyclical issued on 24 June, A.D. 1888, demonstrate

his fatherly concern for the Irish people, despite the mixed reactions

these actions elicited amid the land agitation.

Papal Influence in America

Pope Leo XIII consistently admired the United States, and

his actions demonstrated his deep engagement with the country. He

confirmed the decrees of the *Third Plenary Council of Baltimore*[177] in

A.D. 1884 and elevated Archbishop Gibbons of Baltimore to the

---

[177] **The Third Plenary Council of Baltimore:** held in A.D. 1884, was the most significant of the three plenary councils convened in the United States. It standardized Catholic education, mandated the establishment of parochial schools, and issued the Baltimore Catechism, which shaped Catholic instruction for generations of American Catholics.

[Third Plenary Council of Baltimore. *Acts and Decrees of the Third Plenary Council of Baltimore.* (Baltimore: John Murphy Company, A.D. 1886).]

cardinalate in A.D. 1886. His favorable stance toward the *Knights of Labor,*[178] influenced by Cardinal Gibbons, earned him widespread approval in A.D. 1888.

In 1889, Pope Leo sent Monsignor Satolli as his papal delegate to Washington, representing him at the foundation of the Catholic University of America. The Apostolic Delegation in Washington was officially established in 1892, and the same year saw the publication of his Encyclical on Christopher Columbus.

Pope Leo's involvement in commemorating the discovery of America continued in 1893, when he contributed valuable relics to the Chicago Exposition and sent Monsignor Satolli as his representative. In 1895, he addressed the U.S. hierarchy with his memorable Encyclical *Longinqua Oceani Spatia*, and in 1898, he issued the letter *Testem Benevolentiæ* to Cardinal Gibbons regarding the issue of "Americanism." He also responded with an admirable letter in

---

[178] **Knights of Labor:** founded in A.D. 1869, the Knights of Labor were one of the first major American labor organizations. Under the leadership of Terence V. Powderly, it sought to unite all workers—regardless of trade, race, or gender—under a broad platform of labor reform. Though controversial among some Church authorities for its secrecy and radicalism, it received papal approval in the United States largely due to the advocacy of Cardinal James Gibbons.
> [Weir, Robert E. *Beyond Labor's Veil: The Culture of the Knights of Labor.* (University Park, PA: Pennsylvania State University Press, A.D. 1996), pp. 93-95).]

1902 to the American hierarchy, acknowledging their congratulations on his papal jubilee.

In Canada, Pope Leo confirmed the A.D. 1889 agreement with the Province of Quebec, which resolved the Jesuit Estates question. In A.D. 1897, he sent Monsignor Merry del Val to negotiate with the Canadian Government regarding the contentious Manitoba School Law.

Pope Leo's legacy also endures in South America, particularly for the First Plenary Council of Latin America held in Rome in A.D. 1899, as well as for his noble Encyclical to the bishops of Brazil in A.D. 1888, which called for the complete abolition of slavery, echoing several centuries of previous popes in their condemnation of slavery around the world.

Diplomatic Engagements

Pope Leo XIII achieved notable diplomatic successes during his papacy. In Portugal, the government ceased supporting the *Goan schism*,[179] and in A.D. 1886, a concordat was drawn up. This was

---

[179] **The Goan Schism:** (A.D. 1838–1886), arose when the Portuguese government refused to recognize the authority of bishops appointed by the Holy See in India, particularly in Goa, favoring instead the Padroado system of royal patronage. This resulted in a prolonged ecclesiastical division between pro-Rome and pro-Portugal

followed by concordats with Montenegro in A.D. 1886 and

Colombia in A.D. 1887. Additionally, the Sultan of Turkey, the Shah

of Persia, the Emperors of Japan and China (A.D. 1885), and the

Negus of Abyssinia, Menelik, all sent royal gifts to the pope, who

reciprocated with gifts of his own.

Pope Leo's charitable efforts also extended to the diplomatic

arena. His intervention on behalf of Italian prisoners captured during

the unfortunate Battle of Adwa (A.D. 1898) with the Negus of

Abyssinia was unsuccessful, due to the attitude of those who should

have been most grateful.

His attempts to establish direct diplomatic relations with the

Sublime Porte (Ottoman Empire) and China were thwarted by the

jealousy of France, which feared losing its protectorate over

Christians. During the negotiations regarding church property in the

Philippines, Mr. William Howard Taft, later President of the United

States, had the opportunity to witness Pope Leo's exceptional

qualities, as he later attested on a memorable occasion.

---

factions. Pope Leo XIII resolved the dispute through a concordat with Portugal in
A.D. 1886, which reestablished hierarchical unity under papal authority.
[Souza, Teotonio R. de. *Goa to Me*. (New Delhi: Concept Publishing
Company, A.D. 1994), pp. 76–79.]

Papal Position on Italy and Church Initiatives

Pope Leo XIII upheld the stance of his predecessor, Pius IX, regarding the Kingdom of Italy, confirming the ideas he had expressed in his pastoral of A.D. 1860. He advocated for the complete independence of the Holy See, with its restoration as a true sovereignty. When distressing incidents occurred in Rome, Pope Leo repeatedly sent notes to various governments, pointing out the intolerable situation in which the Holy See found itself due to its subjection to a hostile power.

For this reason, he supported the "Non expedit"—the prohibition against Italian Catholics participating in political elections. His belief was that by abstaining from voting, Catholics would allow subversive elements in Italy to gain power, thus forcing the Italian Government to come to terms with the Holy See. However, events proved him mistaken, and this stance was eventually abandoned by Pius X.

At one point, "officious" negotiations between the Holy See and the Italian Government were conducted through Monsignor Carini, Prefect of the Vatican Library and a close friend of Italian Prime Minister Francesco Crispi. The exact nature of these negotiations remains unclear, but it is known that Crispi was not willing to cede any territory to the Holy See. Furthermore, France, angered by Italy's involvement in the Triple Alliance, intervened to prevent any rapprochement between the Vatican and the Italian Government. Fearing that such an alliance would enhance Italy's prestige, France threatened to renew hostilities against the Church, forcing Pope Leo to break off the negotiations. After Monsignor Carini's death on June 25, A.D. 1895, rumors circulated that he had been poisoned, though this claim remains unfounded.

Pope Leo was equally diligent in promoting the interior life of the Church. To foster piety among the faithful, he recommended the Third Order of St. Francis in A.D. 1882, modifying its rules in A.D. 1883. He instituted the feast of the Holy Family in A.D. 1892, urging that societies in its honor be established worldwide. Many of his encyclicals emphasized the benefits of the Rosary, and he strongly encouraged devotion to the Sacred Heart of Jesus.

Progress of the Catholic Faith

Under Pope Leo XIII, the Catholic Faith experienced significant growth. During his pontificate, two hundred and forty-eight episcopal or archiepiscopal sees were created, along with forty-eight vicariates or Apostolic prefectures. Special attention was given to Catholics of Oriental rites, and Pope Leo had the fortunate opportunity to witness the resolution of the schism that had arisen in A.D. 1870 between the Uniat Armenians. This schism was resolved in A.D. 1879 with the conversion of Mgr. Kupelian and several other schismatic bishops.

Pope Leo founded a college in Rome for Armenian ecclesiastical students in A.D. 1884, and by dividing the College of St. Atanasio, he was able to establish a separate college for the Ruthenians. In A.D. 1882, he had already reformed the Ruthenian Order of St. Basil. For the Chaldeans, he established a seminary at Mossul, which was entrusted to the care of the Dominicans.

In his memorable encyclical *Satis Cognitum* of A.D. 1897, Pope Leo called upon all the schismatics of the East to return to the Universal Church. He also laid down guidelines for managing relations between the various rites in countries with mixed rites. Even among the Copts, his efforts toward reunion made notable progress.

Advancement of Ecclesiastical Sciences

Pope Leo XIII was a generous patron of ecclesiastical sciences. His Encyclical *Æterni Patris* (A.D. 1880) recommended the study of *Scholastic philosophy*,[180] particularly the work of St. Thomas Aquinas, although he cautioned against a servile approach to learning. In Rome, he established the Apollinare College, a higher institute focused on Latin, Greek, and Italian classics. At his suggestion, a Bohemian college was also founded in Rome. Additionally, in Anagni, he founded and entrusted to the Jesuits a college to serve all the dioceses of the Roman Campagna, a model for the provincial or "regional" seminaries later desired by Pius X.

Historical scholars owe much to Pope Leo for opening the Vatican Archives in A.D. 1883. On this occasion, he published an eloquent encyclical emphasizing the importance of historical studies, asserting that the Church had nothing to fear from historical truth.

---

[180] **Scholastic Philosophy:** which reached its zenith in the 13th-century A.D. with figures such as St. Thomas Aquinas, sought to reconcile faith and reason through rigorous dialectical method rooted in Aristotelian logic. It dominated medieval university curricula and shaped Catholic theological thought for centuries. Though its influence waned during the Renaissance and Enlightenment, Scholasticism remained a foundational framework in seminary education and was officially revived in the late-19th-century A.D. by the Catholic Church.
[Copleston, Frederick. *A History of Philosophy, Vol. 2: Medieval Philosophy – Augustine to Scotus.* (New York: Image Books, A.D. 1993), pp. 204–211.]

For the administration of the Vatican Archives and Library, he

enlisted eminent scholars such as Hergenröther, Denifle, and Ehrle;

he also attempted to recruit Janssen, though the latter declined,

preferring to complete his *History of the German People*. To assist

students of the archives and library, Pope Leo established a

consulting library.

The Vatican Observatory stands as another great achievement

of Pope Leo XIII. To encourage Catholic students to rival non-

Catholics in Biblical studies and guide their research, he published the

Providentissimus Deus (A.D. 1893), which garnered admiration even

from Protestants. In A.D. 1902, he also established a Biblical

Commission. Furthermore, in response to the growing influence of

Kantism[181] and *Modernism*,[182] Pope Leo warned the French clergy in his

---

[181] **Kantism:** denotes the philosophical system of Immanuel Kant, especially his claim that the human mind structures experience through innate categories, thereby limiting knowledge to phenomena and excluding metaphysical realities (e.g., God, the soul) from rational demonstration. This epistemological turn profoundly influenced modern philosophy and theological debates concerning reason and revelation.

[Kant, Immanuel. *Critique of Pure Reason*, trans. Paul Guyer and Allen W. Wood. (Cambridge: Cambridge University Press, A.D. 1998), pp. 178-179.]

[182] **Modernism:** in a Catholic theological context, refers to a movement that sought to reconcile Church teaching with modern philosophical currents, historical-critical biblical scholarship, and evolving cultural norms. It often emphasized subjective religious experience and was seen by the Church as undermining traditional dogma and ecclesiastical authority.

A.D. 1899 encyclical *Au Milieu* and, prior to that, addressed the dangers of "*Americanism*"[183] in a brief to Cardinal Gibbons (22 January, A.D. 1899).

Pope Leo definitively ruled against the validity of Anglican orders in his Brief *Apostolicæ Curæ* (A.D. 1896). Throughout his pontificate, he issued several important encyclicals addressing the most pressing issues of modern society. These documents are renowned for their classical style, clarity, and logical persuasion. Notable among them are: *Arcanum divinæ sapientiæ* (A.D. 1880) on Christian marriage; *Diuturnum illud* (A.D. 1881) and *Immortale Dei* (A.D. 1885) on Christianity as the foundation of political life; *Sapientiæ christianæ* (A.D. 1890) on the duties of a Christian citizen; *Libertas* (A.D. 1888) on the true meaning of liberty; and *Humanum genus* (A.D. 1884) against Freemasonry, along with other related

---

[O'Connell, Marvin R. *Criticisms of the Enlightenment: Catholicism and the Challenge of Modernity.* (New York: Herder and Herder, A.D. 1969), pp. 45-47.]

[183] **Americanism:** describes a set of tendencies among certain late-19th-century A.D. American Catholics that promoted adaptation to liberal democratic ideals, personal conscience, and activism over hierarchical obedience and doctrinal uniformity. Though its proponents denied heterodoxy, the movement was officially cautioned against by the Vatican for appearing to dilute Catholic tradition.

[McAvoy, Thomas T. *The Great Crisis in American Catholic History, 1895–1900.* (Chicago: Henry Regnery Company, A.D. 1957), pp. 1-3.]

documents.

Advancement of Ecclesiastical Sciences

Civilization owes much to Pope Leo XIII for his stance on the social question. As early as A.D. 1878, in his encyclical on the equality of all men, he addressed the fundamental error of Socialism. His Encyclical *Rerum Novarum* (18 May, A.D. 1891) offered a profound examination of Christian principles regarding the relations between capital and labor, giving a vigorous impulse to the social movement along Christian lines. Particularly in Italy, this sparked an intense, well-organized movement. However, over time, dissensions emerged. Some factions leaned too heavily towards Socialism, interpreting the term "Christian Democracy" in a political context, while others swung to the opposite extreme.

In A.D. 1901, Pope Leo issued the Encyclical *Graves de Communi*, which aimed to resolve the controversial points surrounding this issue of Christian Democracy. The *Catholic Action*[184]

---

[184] **Catholic Action:** was a lay movement in the Catholic Church that sought to bring the principles of the faith into public life through non-political, religious, and social engagement, particularly in response to the rise of secular ideologies in the 19th- and early 20th-centuries A.D.

    [Charles, Rodger. *Catholic Social Teaching 1891–Present.* (Ignatius Press, A.D. 1998), pp. 80–84.]

movement in Italy was recognized, and the *Opera dei Congressi*[185] was expanded with the creation of a second group focused on economic-social action. Unfortunately, this latter movement did not endure, and Pius X was compelled to create a new party that has yet to overcome its internal challenges.

Religious Orders

Under Pope Leo XIII, religious orders flourished remarkably. New orders were established, older ones expanded, and within a short time, they had made up for the losses caused by unjust spoliation. In every area of religious and educational activity, these orders played a significant role in awakening and strengthening the Christian life across the country. For their better guidance, wise constitutions were issued, and reforms were enacted. Orders such as the Franciscans and Cistercians, which had previously fragmented into separate sections, were reunited. Additionally, the Benedictines

---

[185] **The Opera dei Congressi:** (Works of the Congresses), was an Italian Catholic lay organization founded in A.D. 1874 to promote Catholic social, cultural, and political involvement; it played a central role in organizing Catholic Action before being dissolved by Pius X in A.D. 1904 due to internal conflicts and increasing politicization.

[Pollard, John. *The Vatican and Italian Fascism, 1929–32: A Study in Conflict.* (Cambridge University Press, A.D. 1985), pp. 20.]

were granted an abbot-primate, who resides at St. Anselm's College, founded in Rome under Pope Leo's patronage in A.D. 1883. Rules were also established for members of religious orders who had become secularized.

Canon Law

In canon law, Pope Leo XIII did not make radical changes, yet his vigilant oversight ensured that no part of it escaped his attention. He made timely modifications to meet the evolving needs of the times. Overall, his twenty-five-year pontificate was one of the most externally successful in the Church's history. This success was, in part, facilitated by the general peace between nations. The people, weary of the anticlericalism that had led governments to neglect their primary duty—the well-being of the governed—found Leo's approach appealing. Meanwhile, prudent statesmen feared excessive concessions to elements that threatened the stability of society. Pope Leo himself made every effort to avoid conflict. His three jubilees— the golden jubilees of his priesthood and episcopate, and the silver jubilee of his pontificate—demonstrated the broad popular support he enjoyed. His appearances at Vatican receptions or in St. Peter's always sparked enthusiastic outbursts from the crowd. Despite being far from robust in health, Leo's methodical and regular lifestyle helped him persevere. He was a tireless worker, often demanding exceptional effort from those who worked alongside him. While the conditions of the Holy See did not allow him to do much for art, he did oversee the renewal of the apse of the Lateran Basilica, the rebuilding of its presbytery, and the commissioning of paintings for several halls in the Vatican.

Encyclicals and His Vision

Pope Leo XIII was a remarkably prolific writer, issuing eighty-five encyclicals during his twenty-five-year pontificate—the most of any pope to date. These documents addressed a vast range of topics, including theology, philosophy, education, politics, and social justice. Through his encyclicals, Leo XIII laid the intellectual groundwork for much of modern Catholic social teaching and helped reinvigorate Thomism as a guiding framework for Catholic intellectual life. His writings displayed not only a deep concern for the spiritual welfare of the Church but also a keen awareness of the political and cultural shifts of the modern world.

Pope Leo XIII

Beyond his public teaching, Pope Leo XIII is also remembered for a mystical experience that left a lasting mark on Catholic devotional life. According to accounts circulated in the Vatican, one day after celebrating Mass in A.D. 1884, Leo collapsed into what witnesses believed was a trance or moment of intense spiritual focus. When he awoke, visibly shaken, he reportedly recounted a terrifying vision in which Satan appeared before God and boasted that he could destroy the Church if given greater power over it. Christ, in turn, granted him permission to test the Church for a period of one hundred years. Deeply moved by this experience, Leo XIII composed the Prayer to Saint Michael the Archangel, instructing that it be recited after every Low Mass throughout the Catholic world—a custom that endured well into the 20th-century A.D.

This episode, whether interpreted literally or as symbolic of Leo's deep spiritual concerns, reflects the seriousness with which he regarded the threats facing the Church in the modern age—rationalism, secularism, socialism, and moral relativism. Yet Pope Leo XIII remained unwavering in hope. He viewed the Church not as a relic of the past, but as a living body, divinely protected yet humanly responsible, called to illuminate a darkening world with the light of

The Legacy of Pope Leo

reason and grace. His legacy endures not only in papal documents and institutional reforms but in the spirit of thoughtful engagement with the modern world that continues to animate Catholic life today. He died on July 20, A.D. 1903, after reigning for 25 years.

Pope Leo XIII

St. Michael the Archangel Prayer

Saint Michael the Archangel,

defend us in battle.

Be our protection against the wickedness and snares of the devil.

May God rebuke him, we humbly pray;

and do thou, O Prince of the heavenly host,

by the power of God,

cast into hell Satan and all the evil spirits

who prowl about the world

seeking the ruin of souls. **Amen.**

Chapter XIV

Pope Leo XIV (A.D. 2025-Present)

The First American Pope

Pope Leo XIV, born Cardinal Robert Francis Prevost, made history as the first American pope in the history of the Catholic Church. Elected on May 8, A.D. 2025, he ascended to the papacy during a period marked by significant internal and external challenges for the Church. Born in the United States in A.D. 1955, Cardinal Prevost's early life was deeply shaped by faith and devotion. Raised in a devout Catholic family, his path to the priesthood seemed almost destined. After completing his seminary studies, he was ordained a priest in A.D. 1981 and quickly distinguished himself as a compassionate and visionary leader. His dedication to pastoral care, combined with intellectual rigor, earned him wide respect within the American clergy.

Pope Leo XIV

Cardinal Prevost's rise to the papacy was gradual yet steady. He was appointed bishop in A.D. 2003 and elevated to cardinal in A.D. 2016. His work transcended local boundaries, as he took on significant roles within the Vatican, particularly in liturgy and Church governance. Known for deep prayer and scholarly conviction, he became recognized for bridging ideological divides. His tenure as a cardinal was marked by active involvement in the Synod of Bishops and a firm commitment to ecumenism, dialogue, and social justice.

Just days after his election, Pope Leo XIV explained that he chose his papal name primarily in honor of Pope Leo XIII, whose encyclical *Rerum Novarum* on Catholic social teaching had deeply inspired him. This choice underscored his dedication to continuing the mission of addressing social justice and workers' rights within the framework of Catholic doctrine.

By adopting the name Leo, he signaled both a respect for tradition and a commitment to a forward-looking vision of the Church—one that balances faithful adherence to the past with compassionate engagement with contemporary challenges. His election has been widely seen as a pivotal moment, marking a new chapter that honors the rich heritage of the papacy while embracing the growing global nature of the Church in the 21st-century A.D.

The significance of Pope Leo XIV's American origin cannot be overstated. The United States exerts immense political, economic, and cultural influence over the Western world, yet this influence has increasingly diverged from traditional Christian values. Across the West, birth rates have collapsed due to materialsim, abortion, and artifical birth control, and Christianity has been in marked decline. The U.S. stands at the epicenter of many modern social and moral crises, including widespread religious indifferentism, the proliferation of Protestant heresies, the rise of feminism, high divorce rate, unchecked capitalism contributing to urban decay, and a dependence on foreign labor under exploitative conditions for cheap products.

Moreover, cultural shifts have normalized lifestyles and practices—such as homosexuality, transgenderism, abortion, in vitro fertilization (IVF), and euthanasia—that depart significantly from historic Christian teachings. The digital age has compounded these issues, fostering isolation and enabling the growth of online pornography, prostitution, and human trafficking. Disturbing trends include wealthy homosexual couples commissioning disadvantaged women to bear children, only to separate these children from their mothers and raise them in these perverse households. Pope Leo XIV inherits the daunting task of guiding a Church and a world enmeshed in these profound moral and spiritual crises, and his American roots uniquely position him at the intersection of confronting these challenges head-on.

As this new chapter in the papacy unfolds, Pope Leo XIV stands as a symbol of continuity and renewal—a leader rooted in tradition yet acutely aware of the urgent need for the Church to address the pressing realities of the modern world. Across much of the West, mass attendance has sharply declined, and belief in the true presence of Christ in the Eucharist has significantly waned, reflecting a broader crisis of faith and identity. Yet amid these challenges, there is reason for hope. Younger generations are beginning to experience the stirrings of a religious revival, expressing a renewed thirst for order, tradition, and a deeper relationship with Christ.

Pope Leo XIV's journey—from a devout American upbringing to the highest office of the Catholic Church—mirrors the evolving nature of the global Church itself. The challenges before him are formidable, but so too is the enduring strength of faith, reason, and the Church's mission to bring light into the darkest corners of human experience. In the face of uncertainty and change,

the hope remains that through wisdom, courage, and unwavering

devotion, the Church will continue to be a beacon of truth and

salvation for generations to come.

www.ingramcontent.com/pod-product-compliance
Lightning Source LLC
La Vergne TN
LVHW091215080426
835509LV00009B/1009